PRAISE FOR *EVEN WHEN*

"Sara shows us that even when we muddle through all the even whens the universe holds, our God is with us in the muddle. The prose of Sara's personal stories impacts the reader the way great poetry does as she kindly, gently turns our focus to God. God there. Holding us. Loving us. Even when."

Elinor Young — International Speaker and Author of
Award-Winning Memoir *Running on Broken Legs*

"*Even When* by Sara Cormany is a devotional treasure written with beautiful vulnerability because the author knows the reality of difficult days. We all will face difficulties, and her words will help us remember that being brave when life is hard isn't about our strength but is all about the love that walks with us through all the difficult days in life."

Debbie Alsdorf — Author of *Ten Minutes
With God*, *The Faith Dare*, and *Deeper*

"Like Jesus, Sara Cormany understands sorrow, pain, and disappointment. She has been weighed down by the burdens of grief and physical infirmity. God has brought her through some of the darkest valleys imaginable. And instead of cocooning herself in solitude, she breaks herself open on behalf of others. She shows the hurt and the mess and the frailty. Are you hurting? Have you experienced loss? Is chronic illness part of your story? Find peace in these pages. Even when life hurts more than you could have previously conceived, know this: you are not alone."

Becky Antkowiak — Executive Director
of the 540 Writers Community

"I've discovered that none of our life experiences go to waste. God will use all of them if we let Him. Sara Cormany is proof of that. In *Even When: Experiencing God's Presence During Difficult Days*, she's taken what she's learned from God's Word and from numerous difficult circumstances in her own life to encourage and inspire the rest of us. I highly recommend this book!"

Michelle Cox — Bestselling Author of *Hope That Endures, Our Daily Biscuit: Devotions with a Drawl* and the *When Calls The Heart* Devotional Series

"*Even When* by Sara Cormany is a book to cherish. The author's stories, set in an unmovable foundation of biblical truth, provide a tangible reminder that God is always with us. So much more than another book of devotions, these pages are filled with grit and grace, providing a beacon to help others navigate difficult times. This is a book I'll keep on my bedside table, with extras tucked away so I can share it with those struggling through life's challenges."

Edie Melson — Director of the Blue Ridge Mountains
Christian Writers Conference and Award-
Winning Author of the *Soul Care* Series

EVEN
WHEN

SARA CORMANY

EVEN WHEN

by

SARA CORMANY

Experiencing God's Presence During Difficult Days

40 Devotions

DEXTERITY
NASHVILLE

604 Magnolia Lane
Nashville, TN 37211

Published in association with the literary agency: The Blythe Daniel Agency, Inc.

Printed in the United States of America.

First edition: 2024

10 9 8 7 6 5 4 3 2 1

ISBN: 978-1-947297-76-0 (Paperback)
ISBN: 978-1-947297-77-7 (E-book)

Publisher's Cataloging-in-Publication Data

Names: Cormany, Sara, author. | Southerland, Mary, foreword author.
Title: Even when : experiencing God's presence during difficult days / Sara Cormany; foreword by Mary Southerland.
Description: Nashville, TN: Dexterity, 2024.
Identifiers: ISBN: 9781947297760 (paperback) | 9781947297777 (ebook)
Subjects: LCSH Christianity–Prayers and devotions. | Grief–Religious aspects–Christianity. | Bereavement–Religious aspects–Christianity. | Loss (Psychology)–Religious aspects–Christianity. | BISAC Religion / Christian Living / Devotional | Self-Help / Personal Growth / Happiness | Family & Relationships / Death, Grief, Bereavement Classification: LCC BV245. C67 2024 | DDC 242/.8–dc23

Cover design by Charissa Newell at twolineSTUDIO.
Interior design by Lapiz.

To the ones who hold my heart . . .
Nathan, Grace, Drew, Sophia, and Maddie

. . . and to the ones who are waiting to welcome me Home.

CONTENTS

FOREWORD

I have known Sara Cormany for many years, and I can honestly say that she is the real deal. I have seen her face and conquer circumstances that would bring most people to their knees in painful defeat. Not Sara. I have watched her face each one of the many trials with an insatiable joy and a childlike trust in God. It is almost unbelievable to watch her use every painful situation to point the people in her world back to what many might not see as a loving God. I mean, how could He allow so many horrific things happen to His precious daughter? I have a nickname for Sara. *Jobetta.* Because to me she is the female version of Job. She really should have a reality television show because you just can't make up the things that have happened to Sara.

I am truly in awe of this woman!

And now, through this incredible book, you can catch a glimpse of the world through her eyes. And let me tell you, it is a very different world according to Sara. Each word in this absurdly poignant book is true. Sara is authentic, transparent, and delights in turning painful circumstances into opportunities to praise God, knowing He will take every one of those messy, broken pieces and frame them into a work of art. It is such an honor to endorse this book. It may be Sara's first book, but it certainly won't be her last.

As you begin reading *Even When*, you will immediately find yourself drawn into Sara's often chaotic but always adventurous life. Sara beautifully shapes each life experience with delightful humor and piercing truth. She is simply a word master. You will laugh, cry, and find yourself wanting more . . . more of Sara's incredible insight into Scripture and wisdom beyond her years.

Even When is perfect for both personal and small group study. Women will identify with Sara through these pages as they learn how to trust God even when it makes no sense, even when it is painful, even when you just don't want any more experiences to strengthen your faith. You may be satisfied with where you are in your walk with God, but *Even When* will make you hunger for a new depth of understanding of just who God is and wants to be in your life. Now grab a cup of coffee and turn the first page with expectancy. You are about to encounter God in a whole new way. Blessings!

Mary Southerland
International Author and Speaker
Founding Member, Girlfriends in God

A NOTE FROM THE AUTHOR

I never meant to be a writer.

But twelve years ago, when our little world fell down and life felt tenuous at best, the page became a place where I met Jesus— where He and I dug through all the hard, the tear-stained, and (often) the utterly ridiculous pieces of our lives.

Those words on a page served as a reminder that God would be everything we needed as I struggled to reconcile our future with the backdrop of a stroke and life-altering septic miscarriage. In many ways, those written words provided a safety that the spoken word could no longer offer. But in every way, they pulled our hearts back to the goodness of God and His unending grace.

Even when we failed.
Even when we raged.
Even when we questioned.
Even when we faceplanted on the floor.

His grace was enough.

While I cannot promise this book will be life changing, I can promise it will be real.

Each story found here serves as a reminder that God is not only worthy of our trust, but He is also right beside us on days that steal our breath and break our hearts.

From our journey as newlyweds fighting a chronic illness no one understood. To walking away from my dream of being a teacher because of a body that could not keep up. To Sharpie on the walls, poop on the floor, and the highs and lows of motherhood. To a stroke and a subsequent life-threatening illness. To the mundane humdrum of everyday living. To the people who bravely walked into our messiness. And to the loss of those we've loved along the way.

This is our story. This is our hard stuff. This is how we found Him present in it.

Devotion 1

EVEN WHEN WE WANT TO HOLD ON, HE HELPS US TO LET GO

Verse: "You hem me in, behind and before, and lay your hand upon me." Psalm 139:5

My husband's arms carried me up the stairs to my classroom one last time. After he set me down, I steadied my gait and made my way to the chalkboard with hands shaking, heart pounding.

It seemed like an impossible ending: walking away from my dream, my students, my classroom, surrendering to an illness no one understood, leaving it all behind, unfinished and undone at barely twenty-six.

Forcing me to say goodbye to a place where I had learned about life and love. A place where I had seen His goodness poured out. A place where my heart felt at home.

I could stay. I should stay. I would stay, I told myself.

But then she appeared in the doorway—our tiny, tough-as-nails building secretary. Without a word, she took my hand. Her eyes saw every bit of weakness, every piece of struggle. And her hands gently led me to a place where we could sit eye-to-eye.

"Baby girl, it's time to let go."

I choked back through my tears, "But this is breaking my heart . . ."

"I know, baby girl. That's why I'm here to help you."

Her strength steadied my hands just enough so my heart could follow. I turned back to the chalkboard, scribbled out what remained to be said to my students, gathered all the little things I called mine, and readied myself to say goodbye.

She then took my hand and prayed truth and grace over my weary heart, giving me just enough courage to hobble out the door and into the arms of the man who would carry me home.

This is how we surrender a dream: With hands shaking. With tears falling. With hearts breaking.

We might walk away from something that has long held our hearts. Or we might let go of something we only hoped for today. Yet we know we can surrender it all because we trust the One who sees us, the One who sits with us, the One who draws us near and mercifully whispers, "Baby girl, it's time to let go."

Questions: When have you surrendered a dream? Whom has God brought to you in those seasons to help you let go? How can you be that person for someone else?

Prayer: Father, we come before You with our broken and shattered dreams. May our hearts bend into the extravagance of Your grace. May we know Your peace even as our hands shake. And may we live boldly in the truth that You are forever and always enough. Amen.

Devotion 2

EVEN WHEN OUR BODIES FAIL, HE HEALS OUR HEARTS

Verse: "O Lord my God, I cried to you for help, and you have healed me." Psalm 30:2

I was about to enjoy a beautiful Sunday brunch with my grandparents when I noticed a stranger making a beeline for me in her wheelchair.

Her eyes sparkled. Her silver hair was tucked neatly into a bun. And her bright, flowered dress stood out from the equally silver-haired crowd.

I had barely pushed my chair from the table to get myself something to eat when she arrived. But soon, we were chatting and laughing and swapping teacher stories as if old friends. When my empty stomach reminded me I still hadn't eaten, I began to stand once again . . .

And then she saw it: my ever so lovely assistive device. As we made our way to the food line together, she said, "I hope you don't mind me asking, but why do you walk with a cane?"

With a shrug and half-smile, I gave her the quick answer, "A stroke."

But she pressed for more and more and more, and by the end, I had told her everything. About the autoimmune disease. The stroke. The miscarriage. The septic shock. The rainbow baby. The blood clot. The lung issues. The heart complications. The surgeries. The whole big mess and a half.

I watched as her eyes widened with each new thing. But as I drew to a close, she said something I will never forget: "What incredible healing you've had!"

No, "I'm sorry." No, "Whoa, that's a lot." No, "I can't believe you have been through so much!" Instead, all she offered was a baffled look and, "What incredible healing you've had!"

It wasn't until I rode home with my loves that I sat under the full grace of her words.

Little did I know that two weeks later I would be hospitalized with severe sepsis and pneumonia in both lungs. Little did I know that my recovery would last months and months.

Little did I know that I would be back in a place I have been so many times before—a place where both my heart and my body would encounter Jehovah Rapha, my Healer.

A place where I would accept the grace of what He has done over and over again. With gratitude to a God who loves me so much that He would fight for me and send someone whose voice would echo across my life on that day and the days that followed: "What incredible healing you've had!"

Questions: Where has God given you healing in a way the world might ignore? In what ways can you live within the depth of that healing? How can you move forward to find the grace of a new perspective?

Prayer: Father, may we never lose sight of the healing You've already given. May we hold our lives and our expectations open to the possibility of something more. And may we live within a place of hard-won gratitude that comes from placing our full trust in You. Amen.

Devotion 3

EVEN WHEN LIFE OVERWHELMS US, HE GRANTS US PEACE

Verse: "And the peace of God, which surpasses all understanding, will guard your hearts and your minds in Christ Jesus." Philippians 4:7

Not quite two weeks after I delivered my second child, armed with little but hormones and mommy guilt, I stopped at a little pizza joint with my eldest in tow. We had frequented this place so often during my pregnancy, my final weight balloon could safely be credited to their "Slice and a Drink" special.

We laughed. We cried. We bonded.

OK, maybe that's stretching it a bit. I was sleep deprived and she was two. But as we walked out hand in hand, I felt like a rock star mom.

That is, until a kitten ran out into the street.

Before I could breathe a word, her hand left mine and she began chasing after the little streak of gray and white. Above the street noise, I could hear her sweet voice repeating over and over, "Nice kitty. Nice kitty." And even though I couldn't see it, I could hear a car barreling down the road.

Barreling straight toward my baby.

Throwing our leftover pizza box in the air and running as fast as my postpartum legs could carry me, I screamed, "Grace, run to Mama." Her precious face turned toward mine, and I caught her hand just as the tires screeched in front her.

With my heart pounding and tears flowing, I scooped up my girl and nearly hugged the breath out of her. I kissed her face all the way to the car and whispered prayers of gratitude as I sat in my seat waiting for my hands to stop shaking.

The memory of that day has faded with time, but there is one picture seared into my mind's eye: the moment Grace turned. Even with more than a ton of metal coming straight at her, her eyes locked on mine.

She wasn't anxious. Or nervous. Or afraid.

Instead, a quiet confidence filled her big brown eyes. It was as though as long as she had me in her sights, everything was OK. Mom had it under control. Even with me screaming her name, throwing things and losing my ever-loving mind, my girl trusted me.

There was not a bit of sense or logic to it. She displayed not just a peace *within* the circumstance but a peace that *defied* the circumstance.

In the *even whens* of life, this peace has lifted me out of unimaginable sadness and permeated the cruelest of diseases. I have stood in awe at its quiet presence graveside after graveside.

And the reality is: God isn't freaking out or screaming or throwing things. He leaves that crazy business to us. Instead, He calls out softly, just above the street noise.

"Keep your eyes on me, my love, and I'll give you the greatest peace you will ever know."

Questions: When have you taken your eyes off God in exchange for whatever is barreling your way? How can you focus on His presence and guard your heart in the days ahead? How can you trust Him despite your circumstances?

Prayer: Father, may we trust You even when the hard of life threatens to overtake us. May we pray. May we petition. May we praise. And may we do so with a confidence in the peace You so readily offer us in each and every circumstance. Amen.

Devotion 4

EVEN WHEN WE ARE FAITHLESS, HE IS FAITHFUL

Verse: "Now faith is the assurance of things hoped for, the conviction of things not seen." Hebrews 11:1

His smile caught my eye as I whisked up his prayer card one Sunday morning.

With my mama heart already turned to mush, it took little time for our entire family to fall in love with Patrick, a brown-eyed boy in foster care who still needed a forever home.

For weeks, we diligently remembered him at mealtime and bedtime prayers.

But then, as so often happens, I became distracted. Distracted with life, with my own stuff, with my own need for prayer.

Somewhere in all of that distraction, I forgot Patrick. But one person in our house did not. In every bedtime prayer and any in-between, four-year-old Grace remembered.

"God, please help Patrick to find a good home and a good family that loves him."

When she later discovered that Patrick's brother had cerebral palsy, she began to pray for him too.

So it should not have come as a surprise one Sunday morning when she came downstairs with her purple change purse in tow.

I assumed she was trying to sneak in a show-and-tell, even though we'd discussed a thousand times before that no such thing exists at church. I even chastised her. And then she shut down my admonition with one little response.

"But, Mom, I have this quarter that I need to bring to church with me so that I can put it in the offering. It's going to help them find Patrick a good home."

My eyes began to sting a bit as we headed out the door. I had forgotten about Patrick, but Grace and God had not. This little bean was willing to bring all she had to help another. She had faith that if she gave what she had, God could meet the need.

Oh, that we could have faith like that—faith like a child. Faith that even when our offering is small, we believe God can make it much. Faith that not only prays but also acts. Faith that doesn't forget who holds a Father's heart.

I admit I left church that morning less with the memory of any sermon and more with the image of a little girl carefully writing her name on an offering envelope. A few lines down, she scrawled, "For Patrick."

I'm sure those who collected the offering that day wondered what it meant. But the One for whom it was meant understood perfectly.

Questions: Where are you struggling to have faith even in the small things? Where is it hard to forgive yourself for your failures? In what ways can you step forward in faith?

Prayer: Father, may we be reminded that You are bigger, stronger, and greater than anything we could ever face. May we rest in the truth that You are greater, too, than our failings. May we trust You with the smallest of offerings and commit our hearts to knowing You will make it enough. Amen.

Devotion 5

EVEN WHEN WE FEEL DEFEATED, HE GIVES US A REASON TO FIGHT

Verse: "For the Lord comforts Zion; he comforts all her waste places and makes her wilderness like Eden, her desert like the garden of the Lord; joy and gladness will be found in her, thanksgiving and the voice of song." Isaiah 51:3

I can still see her little face turning purple, no doubt choking on something she'd found on the floor.

I would like to say I remained calm and collected, executing the Red Cross standards of airway clearing

without a hitch while we peacefully went on about
our day.

But instead, my baby girl turned purple.

Not because we didn't catch it in time. Not because
I didn't execute RC standards appropriately.

Rather, it happened for one simple reason: my body
failed her.

It was not for lack of trying. As any mama would,
I scooped her up, turned her over, and tried to pound.
But then I lost my grip and nearly dropped her.

Finally, in desperation, I called out to my husband
for help. Dissolving into a blubbering puddle of tears,
I watched while he effortlessly saved our baby.

Nearly forgetting to breathe between sobs, I realized
I needed to pull it together when Grace said, "Mommy,
don't worry, Sophie will go to heaven."

Then she added, "Or I could just pray for a new one . . .
I prayed for Sophie, and that seemed to work."

At this point, my husband gently suggested I might go to the bathroom if I needed to continue losing it everywhere.

A short while later, he came down the stairs with a freshly bathed and perky baby girl. He gently handed her to me and took me in his arms with a tender understanding. I softly whispered as I held her tightly, "I couldn't save her. My body wouldn't let me save her."

After months of denial as to what a weak left side means for a mama with small children, I had come face-to-face with the reality that everyone in my life had tried to impart: my deficit was a danger to my children.

And with my sweet baby being the first one affected, it was just not acceptable.

So as I hobbled into occupational therapy the following morning, I tearfully but forcefully told my therapist what had happened. I apologized for every time I had downplayed her recommendations or fought against them, and I told her, "But I'm ready now."

Wasting no time, she pulled out a giant blue bear. Strapping a weight to his waist, she explained how we would need to practice in a certain way to make the simulation as close as possible to doing the same for Sophie.

I turned, I pounded, I compressed. It was hard. It hurt. But I did it. I even got pretty good at it.

And then my therapist said something I won't ever forget, "See? You just needed a reason to fight."

The irony is that I have seen others experience God making beautiful things from dust. But that day God did so for me. He took the memory of a horrible hue on my little girl's face and turned it into a reason to fight.

Our reason to persevere through difficult seasons might be different, but the beauty God offers us in those seasons is the same. When we invite Him into our struggle, He stands ready to give us what we need or who we need so we can press on and claim the victory that awaits us.

Questions: When has weariness kept you from fighting for something or someone? How has God met you even in those moments? What reasons has He given you to keep pressing onward?

Prayer: Father, may we not grow embittered by that which makes our hearts and bodies weary. May we embrace our hard things, knowing that You bring beauty from them. And may we stand ready to bring You praise for giving us a reason to fight. Amen.

Devotion 6

EVEN WHEN THE WORLD BEGS US TO RUSH, HE ASKS US TO SLOW DOWN

Verse: "I therefore, a prisoner for the Lord, urge you to walk in a manner worthy of the calling to which you have been called, with all humility and gentleness, with patience, bearing with one another in love." Ephesians 4:1-2

The rain hit my face with a vengeance before I lowered it. Glancing at the slick ramp in front of me, I took a deep breath and began to walk.

Heel . . . toe. Heel . . . toe. Heel . . . toe.

I almost didn't notice the gentleman to my right running past me. Or the woman grazing my hand as she dashed to the covered respite in front of us. But as I caught the blurs of movement out of the corner of my eye, a thought occurred to me.

I am learning to live life in slow motion.

Everything is deliberate. Everything is measured. Everything is carefully orchestrated.

Even when it appears to be a fumbling, blessed mess.

Take, for example, the day I decided to go grocery shopping solo with a million produce items on the list. Let me tell you: plastic bags, twist ties, and poor fine motor skills? Surprisingly, they do not mix. Especially when the corn bin's limited selection requires some searching and the fussy folks behind you do not want to wait.

Even as I heard the impatient sighs of those behind me, I did something in that moment that shocked even me. I made them wait.

This world is going at a mind-boggling pace. We don't live in slow-motion but on fast-forward. And usually, I am the fussy one. Fussy that the person in front of me is driving too slowly. Fussy that the cashier made a mistake when my kid is melting down. Fussy that my babies won't hurry up and do what I've said.

Just. Fussy.

But in reality, we know fussy is not what we're supposed to be. Instead, we've been asked to encourage the disheartened, help the weak, be patient with everyone. And that's everyone.

Be it the elderly driver desperately holding onto her freedom, even if patience demands we match her slower pace. Or the three-year-old who longs to be independent but struggles to get his shirt on most days.

What if we had the grace to let them all live in slow motion—bearing with them in love, knowing that one day we'll need that grace too?

And greater still, what if we chose to live in slow motion *with* them? Might that teach us to see God more clearly, know Him more deeply, and experience Him in ways found only in the surrendered and slow?

Questions: How has the world's rushing bred impatience in your spirit? Where can you slow down even in your busyness? How does the way you see others change when you choose to leave rushing behind?

Prayer: Father, may we embrace the grace of going slow. May we set fussy down for the sake of loving others. And may we rest and still our hearts so that we might see the things You show us only in the slow. Amen.

Devotion 7

EVEN WHEN WE FEEL WORTHLESS, HE FINDS US WORTHY

Verse: "In this the love of God was made manifest among us, that God sent his only Son into the world, so that we might live through him." I John 4:9

One night I found unexpected grace in an ER waiting room.

Wrapped up in warm blankets and IV fluids, I faded in and out to the sounds of *Seinfeld*, waiting for the outcome of my CT scans.

I had seen glimmers of grace in that room, circling around frustrated patients and long wait times and not enough beds.

Nurses, aides, and admissions staff all responded with gentleness and concern. I even had to chortle a bit at their unrelenting calm in the chaos.

Calm when a young woman attempted to light up next to an oxygen tank. Calm when the security guard explained to a visitor why pocketknives were, in fact, not allowed in the ER. And calm when the man with ill-fitting drawers lost the battle and they fell straight to the floor.

But it wasn't until I found myself in my hospital room that I understood I had landed in the middle of the most remarkable love story. A story of one man and an entire emergency room staff who loved him.

For four hours I'd heard him curse and yell and rage. And for four hours, I'd heard person after person respond to him with love and kindness and respect.

It was clear the staff knew him well.

Even as one doctor apologized for any disturbance this man may have caused me, I still heard a gentleness in his voice. One that prompted me to ask, "I take it he comes here often?"

With a nod and a smile, he replied, "Sometimes up to two and three times a day. Normally, he has a harmonica that calms him down, but today the harmonica didn't make it."

Somewhere between the smile and the harmonica, I knew this was a grace worth writing about.

Because it showed up every day without expectation of recognition or fanfare. Because it stretched through the ravages of illness to find someone's humanity. Because it stood willingly in places most of us would never dare go.

This is the same grace that stretched out its hand on the cross. This is the grace that brings hope to places dark and unlovely. This is the same grace we can extend if we only open our eyes to see the one truth we cannot deny:

We were all worth a Father's Son.

Questions: Where have you seen God turn toward you even in your anger and pain? How has that experience affected your treatment of others? Where can you use the love He has given you to meet others in their brokenness?

Prayer: Father, may we see the lonely, the lost, and the forgotten. May we offer others what You so graciously have given us: unending mercy, unconditional love, unencumbered kindness. And may we see in everyone what was worth a Father's Son. Amen.

Devotion 8

EVEN WHEN HE CLOSES A DOOR, HE IS WITH US IN THE HALLWAY

Verse: "The Lord is near to the brokenhearted and saves the crushed in spirit." Psalm 34:18

The doors of the elevator closed with a heavy thud.

Hands shaking, I drew my purse close to my chest. Took a deep breath. And counted the floors as we climbed. 1 . . . 2 . . . 3 . . . 4 . . . 5.

Then, just as abruptly as they closed, the doors opened in full view of the welcome desk.

The receptionist was the same. The waiting room was just as bare. And my heart seemed just as heavy.

Strangely enough, even the couple who came out laughing with their sonogram looked just like the couple who came out laughing that day in September.

As my husband settled down in the chair next to mine, I tried to pretend I was reading. Then, just as before, gave up. Opting to stare at the bright pink daisy on the wall until I heard, "Sara?"

I clutched my purse tightly once again and smiled awkwardly at the nurse who led us back through the same hallway.

To my left was the room where I'd faced a silent sonogram. To my right was the man who was there to hold my hand. And in front of us was something else entirely.

More numbers, more impossibilities, and more risks.

In my heart, I wanted to hear that a baby was possible. I had lost a piece of my heart, and now I wanted hope to fill my arms.

But instead, we faced statistics that made it seem impossible. We had to let go of babies and focus on my wreck of a body and all of its challenges.

We heard, "*This* puts you at risk of another stroke. And *this* puts you at risk of this complication. Oh, and this—I guess *this* also puts you at an increased risk of stroke too."

I was done. Tired and deflated.

But when I came home and opened my computer to do something mindless, I found these three words staring back at me: "Is Jesus enough?"

For nearly two hours, I sat wrestling with that line. "Was that really true of me? Was Jesus enough?"

You see, society told me I should have what I want, especially as a mom.

Babies. Comfort. A plan. And all on my terms.

But the truth? Jesus is it. Point blank, it. He's all I've ever needed. And really, deep down in my spirit, He trumps all I've ever wanted.

Only He could have taken my loss by its ugliness, turned it around, and made a way for me to know Him. Fall on my face. Tears streaming down. *Know* Him.

So that afternoon, sitting at my dirty kitchen table, I uttered a quiet prayer.

"Lord, take my empty arms. My wreck of a body. Take it all. Use them for You. Fill them with You. Just You. You're enough. For me. For always. Forever enough."

Questions: Where has life left you wanting? How has Jesus met you even in that wanting? How would you answer the question, "Is Jesus enough?"

Prayer: Father, may we hold our want loosely. May we surrender our earthly emptiness for the sufficiency of who You are. And may we trade our broken for all the ways Your Son has made us whole. Amen.

Devotion 9

EVEN WHEN HARD THINGS TRY TO WEIGH US DOWN, HE USES THEM TO LIFT OTHERS UP

Verse: "Come and hear, all you who fear God, and I will tell what he has done for my soul." Psalm 66:16

I remember the day I knew life with a cane would be ridiculous.

That fateful December night, I, my cane, and my brood were insanely late to rehearsal for the annual children's Christmas choir.

Hilarity began the moment we walked into a room packed with parents but nary a child, and my eldest loudly announced, "See, Mom! I told you we were late."

Sure enough. And the next ten minutes nearly undid me completely. Ten minutes because that was all that was left of rehearsal.

I gradually became unglued by our resident Spiderman—who climbed every table, wall, and chair in the room. And by the toddler flailing on the floor and screaming like a banshee. And by the mere logistical nightmare of attempting to parent one-handed with a cane.

Needless to say, it was a blessedly full ten minutes.

But the very moment rehearsal ended, I grabbed the toddler with my free arm and nearly Hallelujah-chorused my way out of there, praying us toward the elevator. A strategy thwarted when Spiderman started kicking the bottom of my cane and I found myself sweating profusely while trying not to topple over all of them.

But then I heard it.

A snort. A chortle. A guffaw.

I turned to find a fellow mom-warrior, who answered my wild-eyed look with, "I'm sorry, Sara. But this is just so, so, well, ridiculous!"

And without a hint of hesitation, I snorted back "I *know*! Would you please call my PT and doctor and explain what you have just witnessed?"

This is when the child under my arm faceplanted to the floor and I nearly joined her.

Later that evening while downing copious amounts of chocolate, I received a note from another sweet mama who had seen our whole blessed mess and just wanted me to know it made her feel normal in hers.

There, sitting under the glow of Christmas lights with the toddler now cuddled up beside me, I realized something important: I had usually been able to mask my pain or my weakness. But in a horribly awful, beautiful kind of way, this life with a cane and all that came with it was a new kind of testimony.

The truth is, we were never meant to show the world a perfect us. Instead, we were meant to show others what it is to be loved and held by a perfect God. Even on the days when it's a craptastic mess and the world is audience to the entire meltdown.

Because those are the days when God shows others the full measure of His grace, where our weakness becomes the perfect testimony to His strength.

Questions: When has life humbled you? How has God taken that humbling and brought redemption from it? Where can you offer up your mess for His glory?

Prayer: Father, may we come before You with the humility to embrace the suffering that is ours. May we see that what might leave us red-faced and embarrassed may actually breathe grace into the heart of another. And may we see Your purpose in it as bigger and better than our own. Amen.

Devotion 10

EVEN WHEN MOUNTAINS STAND IN OUR WAY, HE MOVES THE IMPOSSIBLE

Verse: "Jesus replied, 'What is impossible with man is possible with God.'" Luke 18:27 NIV

Sporting some oddly fitting stretch pants, I walked into physical therapy one morning determined to knock out my session and skedaddle on home.

But to my surprise, I was met by a young resident with neatly pressed pants and a clear desire to learn.

We were an unlikely pair indeed.

Toss in my physical therapist, who was there to teach, and I was left to be the visual aid.

Or so I thought.

The lesson involved the beloved weighted bear, recently and affectionately named "Baby Sophie" by the staff. My objective? Lean down to lift "Sophie" up from the floor and bring us both to standing position without toppling over.

I can assure you, there is nothing like a bit of bum falling, playing with a giant bear, and sweating uncontrollably to break the getting-to-know-you ice with someone you've just met.

After several unsuccessful attempts, I succeeded, however less-than-ballerina-graceful I appeared.

My PT prefaced the next challenge with, "I'm pretty sure that she will have some problems with this." To which I retorted, "Hey, now!" This caused the two of us to erupt in a fit of giggles, which confused the otherwise serious resident.

Turns out, I failed the oral instruction element miserably. The first leg of the test, which involved walking ten feet and turning my head from side to side, hinged on said oral instruction. Upon her fifth attempt at explanation and my fifth failure of completion, my PT just chuckled as she said, "OK, one more time . . ."

"Processing, processing! This brain. It has trouble with the processing!" I playfully barked back.

Finally, at the end of our session, I was asked to walk down a hallway while counting down from one hundred. A task that made me chortle at the mere explanation. Because I knew it would be a blessed disaster.

And it was.

As difficult as I found the brisk walking, the audible tracking of the numbers was almost outright ridiculous. So much so that a sweet passerby smiled at me and said, "Wow, you are good at math." To which my PT and I loudly guffawed.

Because we knew I was a hot mess.

Sweating yet again, I sat down in a chair to rest from the Olympic feat while my PT explained to the resident how movement and multitasking are incredibly difficult following traumatic brain injury. She ended with, "If we'd sat her in a chair and asked her to do the same thing, she would have had no problems doing it."

In that moment, I realized I was not just the visual aid. I was also the teacher. I was teaching the resident what it meant to have a brain and a body that don't work together.

Truthfully, it was a lesson I wished I didn't have to teach. But sometimes, the greatest lessons come when we least expect them.

I knew that, somewhere in between the snorting and my ill-fitting stretch pants, God had moved a mountain. What had nearly broken me was now building something in me. What had once brought tears and anger now brought joy and laughter. What had been a mountain of insecurity and anguish, He had exchanged for healing.

This is the grace of the impossible. Without God, it's nothing but an obstacle. With God, it's just the beginning of what's possible.

Questions: When has God helped you face what felt impossible? What has He built in you and through you during those seasons? How can you open your eyes and fully experience the grace of the impossible?

Prayer: Father, may we trust You with our impossible. May we see Your strength in the middle of our weakness. And may we walk in the grace that You will work even our hardest moments for our good. Amen.

Devotion 11

EVEN WHEN WE ARE WOUNDED AND WAR-TORN, HE BRINGS OTHERS TO SHARE THE BURDEN

Verse: "Bear one another's burdens, and so fulfill the law of Christ." Galatians 6:2

Somewhere in my fumbling up the stairs I felt a little hand on the small of my back. Landing firmly on my newest scar. Red, bumpy, and just barely healed from a surgeon's scalpel. Not altogether strange for one of my babies to find.

But instead of a quick tap of three-year-old curiosity, her hand stayed put as if she were trying to push me up the stairs in all her toddler strength.

I giggled a bit as I asked, "Whatcha doing, sweets?"

With her usual determination, she clapped back, "I'm just carrying your boo-boos, Mama."

My heart melted a little at her love. She didn't wait for me to ask for help. She simply saw my hurt and jumped in to carry it as if there were nothing to prevent her little frame from doing so.

Even now, I am left with this uncomplicated truth:

Life is filled with boo-boos.

Cuts and scrapes and deep wounds we carry mostly on our own. Fitting so quietly into life we often forget their presence. Quiet until something or someone reminds us of their lumpy, bumped-out existence.

But when we land in mixed up and messy seasons of life, we will all find the evidence of our boo-boos fully on display. We will be brought to a place where the climb is beyond our capacity. We will need the strength and grace of someone else's hand.

Because in every scar's etching, His love will ask us to hold each other up.

To fix firmly on every bumpy piece and not recoil at its ugliness. To walk bravely into the tearstained moments of life even when our hands feel too small. To offer all we are so that someone else won't feel alone in the struggle.

Be it in diagnosis or dreams surrendered or all the places we'd rather not go. He will call us to show up, step in, and remind one another we were never meant to carry hard things alone.

Questions: How has God used the pain of your past to grow strength in your present? When has someone come alongside you to carry your grown-up wounds? How can you come alongside others to do the same?

Prayer: Father, may we offer our scars as holy praise. May we see them as a testament of Your healing and care. May we forge through the pain with perseverance but meet it with equal tenderness, so we can stand ready to meet others in their pain. Amen.

Devotion 12

EVEN WHEN WE ARE WEAK, HE IS STRONG

Verse: "My flesh and my heart may fail, but God is my strength of my heart and my portion forever." Psalm 73:26

I found myself once again in a waiting room—filling out paperwork and preparing to stare down another glitchy brain test.

Feeling every piece of my limitations. In parenthood. In marriage. In friendship.

So much so that I secretly hoped the electrodes they were going to place on my head would magically flip a switch and—"Boom!"—I'd transform from cane-toting mama to superhero. About the time I began picturing myself in a red super suit and cape, two more people walked into the room.

An elderly lady gingerly pushed a walker while her companion walked a few steps ahead. I'd missed the companion's face while engrossed in my superhero day-dreaming. But I could see her gray hair and hear her crackling voice.

"Sweet." I thought. "Must be friends taking care of each other."

But then the receptionist's voice snapped me out of my musing: "Ma'am, your appointment is at 8:00 tomorrow."

"It's tomorra?!" the walker-toting woman cackled loudly. "I mean, really, it's tomorra?"

Joining in with an equally glorious cackle, the other gray-haired love turned in my direction. And just about the time I looked up, she let out an, "Aww, mom." It was then I understood.

The sweet woman with the appointment had Down Syndrome. The giggling gal with her walker was her mama. A mama taking care of her baby, limitation and all.

I found myself wiping away my tears as fast as they fell, just so I could watch them walk out together.

Mama moved slowly and gingerly. Her daughter put her hand on the walker and rested her head on her mama's still giggling shoulders. I could even hear, "Guess we'll just do this again tomorrow, love ..." as the sliding doors slammed shut.

Something in that moment drew my weary heart to stand up to my superhero dreams.

This mama had made it through a lifetime of love. Her body was weaker than her little girl's. But her heart was big enough it didn't matter.

I grabbed greedily at that moment. Held tight to it as I hugged my youngest two later that day. And reminded myself of something I knew all along:

God's love doesn't need a super suit to be real.

We may doubt it in our human need for perfection. We may want it in our need for control. We may long for it in our fear of all that is messy.

But His love will always find a way to remind us that it is in the weakest where His strength grows best.

Questions: Where are your weary and worn-out places? In what ways do you allow them to steal your strength? Where can you praise Him even in your weakness?

Prayer: Father, may you use our worn-out places to love and serve others for eternity's sake. May we hold onto this purpose even in a world bent toward perfection. And may we rejoice in knowing that when we are weak, You are strong. Amen.

Devotion 13

EVEN WHEN WE TURN AWAY, HE PULLS US CLOSE

Verse: "For I, the Lord your God, hold your right hand; it is I who say to you, 'Fear not, I am the one who helps you.'" Isaiah 41:13

Seven months earlier, my sweet daddy had met Jesus. Seven months of me scraping and clawing and hiccupping through waves of emotions. Seven months of learning how to help my babies process their sadness as I clumsily dealt with my own.

Standing at a church service one evening with my daughter, I received the weight of her body and the strength of her embrace as her muffled words fell into my chest: "Mom, I prayed for you tonight, you know, because you've been missing Pop Pop?"

I gently pulled her face up to mine as I quietly answered back, "Oh, sweets, that means everything to me, especially because I know how much you miss him too."

Our words hung there for a beat, and then the swirl of the church crowd swallowed our sadness.

Later that evening, we embraced again. And this time I would not let go even as she flailed and screamed and pounded the breath out of me in her own grief. The more she flailed, the stronger I held. The stronger I held, the more she screamed. Until finally she drew a deep breath, and I sensed it was time to let go.

"I need to be alone now," she said quietly.

And even though my heart broke a little, I gave her one last squeeze and turned and walked away.

An hour passed before she finally came downstairs. She threw her arms around me, kissed me goodnight, and that was that. Or so I thought.

Not a few seconds later, she was back at my side with her arms around me once again, saying, "Thanks."

"For what?"

"For holding me close and not letting go even when my nose was running *everywhere*."

It was with barely a breath that I answered back with another hug, "Oh, honey, that's just what love does."

And even as I heard her head back up the stairs, in the echo of those words my tears began to fall.

How many times in the last seven months had I come to my Jesus with my nose running everywhere? How many times had I screamed a desperate *why* as I flailed in my grief? And how many times had He held me closer and closer and closer until I knew I was so deeply loved that I could not do anything but believe it was true?

I know very little when it comes to the *whys* behind the tough stuff of life. But of this I am absolutely certain:

He is near to the weary, the worn, the overwhelmed, the grief-stricken, and the beat-up. He is balm to the crushed in spirit. He will bind up your wounds and hold you close as you bend toward Him in your brokenness.

He is. He will. He does.

No matter how far you've wandered. No matter how loud you scream. No matter how forcefully you pound.

He will draw you closer until you can finally hear Him say, "This, dear one. *This* is what love does."

Questions: Describe a time God met you in one of your most unlovely moments. How has this helped you comfort others in *their* unlovely moments? In what ways can you surrender your pain for the grace of His embrace?

Prayer: Father, may we taste the goodness of a love that is better than life. May we dwell so deeply there that we cannot help but praise You even at our weakest and most vulnerable. And may we offer ourselves and others the unencumbered beauty of what love does. Amen.

Devotion 14

EVEN WHEN WE MISS THE GIFT OF A NEW DAY, HE GIVES US A REASON TO REJOICE

Verse: "This is the day that the Lord has made; let us rejoice and be glad in it." Psalm 118:24

I could hear my girl saying something as I buckled the baby into the shopping cart.

OK, so it was actually more like yelling, but bless it if I could even tell. I had totally crossed over into the Mom-Zone—when the world could be ending but all you hear is the inner-monologue-of-the-now: "Must get the baby in the seat before a car runs over us."

The consequence of this stealth focus? You agree to anything. And apparently, I had agreed in thirty seconds of nonlistening to sing a rousing rendition of "This Is the Day" while we moseyed through Target.

And while I thought I knew the song, according to my daughter, I did not. Nor could I keep from falling back into the Mom-Zone. Much to my daughter's chagrin and constant correction.

Finally she broke down with, "Mom, I really need you to focus!"

So I got my act together, we found our rhythm, and we did our thang. But alas, when we hit the "together" part of the ditty, things fell apart again. I'm all "This Is the Day," and to my surprise she's all "Jesus Loves Me."

Shortly after this confusion and preciously right as we walked up to an unsuspecting cashier, my girl bellows with ear-piercing volume, "It is not the day the Lord has made!"

And Jesus loves us, this I know.

While the relevance here seems suspect, we all have days where things veer off course and everything we know gets drowned out by our inner monologue of "This is *not* the day the Lord has made!"

And while we can go from blissfully happy to *my day is ruined faster than it takes us to go from the parking lot into a store*, this is the day He has made. And we have the choice to wallow in our ruin or persevere through and count it all joy.

I'm not talking about some kind of false, "Oh, today is magical!" when you are knee deep in poo. I'm talking about being grateful for the gift of a new day. I'm talking about how it's really pretty great to have the chance to sing loudly in the aisles of Target with someone you love.

Because it's in those moments we remember He loves us and has given us a new day. And really?

No matter how you look at it, that is something to sing about.

Questions: Where is your joy dependent on your circumstances? With that in mind, how can you begin to count it all joy no matter the circumstances? How can you persevere toward the grace of a new day?

Prayer: Father, may we see each new day as a gift of Your hands. May we find the riches of Your love undeterred by the day's circumstances. And may we embrace all You have for us and be glad in it. Amen.

Devotion 15

EVEN WHEN WE LOSE OUR WAY, HE CARRIES US ALL THE WAY TO FOUND

Verse: "Make me know the way I should go, for to you I lift up my soul." Psalm 143:8

Once upon a time I got lost. On my way to physical therapy. In a hospital I frequent as much as the grocery store. All courtesy of my wonky brain and the sign that started it all: "Main Parking Garage Full."

A sign I drove by three times before the staff member standing in front of it was reduced to wildly waving and overarticulating, "It is full. Go to the other one."

Well, break my routine and color me confused.

By the time I found the right garage, I was so hopelessly turned around I had been reduced to muttering to myself and breaching any double door I could find in some blind hope PT would be on the other side.

But then I found her, a darling scrub-clad woman who clearly knew I was lost. Made even more obvious when she asked, "Where are you going?" To which I snorted back, "I don't know, do you?"

Laugh. Hoot. Giggle. Wheeze.

Until somewhere in all the merriment, I eked out, "Physical therapy," which made her laugh even harder because I was so not even close. After several rounds of, "Now where do I turn left?" She handed me a map, turned me toward another door and said, "Just keep going!"

But then I somehow ended up in plastic surgery.

Trying to be proactive and avoid the embarrassment of actually walking into an OR, I stopped at the plastic surgery check-in desk and made what I thought was a hilarious joke: "Hey, I'm supposed to go to PT today, but

I thought I'd check to see if I could squeeze a tummy tuck in on my way down?"

The check-in lady was not amused. She gave me a look that clearly said, "This is why I don't work in neuro." And then she pointed her finger toward the direction of the elevator.

Still ever so clueless, I hopped on, pushed G and waited for the door to open. And when it did, there was the waving lady and the sign that had started it all: "Main Parking Garage Full."

Laugh. Hoot. Giggle. Wheeze.

Out of breath and still snorting, I finally found myself in the PT room, my therapist greeting me with a grin. A greeting that launched me into an utterly ridiculous account of my adventures. Only to end with, "But I did it! Forty-five minutes and a few friends later, I did it!"

To which she giggled back "You did. And we're so very glad you're here."

Whew. The mind is a precious gift, y'all. But even more precious is the journey we take.

Sometimes we end up in the oddest of places. Sometimes, we feel like we are a million miles from where we know we need to go. Sometimes, we end up right back where we started, realizing we took the long way Home.

But at the end of the journey, no matter how winded or tired or wounded, no matter how long we've fumbled and sojourned and zig-zagged around, someone waits.

A Father. A Savior. A saint.

Ready to welcome us to the place we truly belong. Ready to hold and heal as we breathlessly exclaim, "I made it!" And ready to answer back, "You did! And we're so very glad you're Home."

Questions: Where are the places in your story where you have felt lost and alone? How has He found you in those places? In what ways can you pursue joy even on the craziest of detours?

Prayer: Father, may we seek You when we find ourselves on roads unnavigated and unknown. May we trust You with our steps. May we ask You for your guidance. And may we move forward confidently, knowing that no matter the road we take, You will be with us from now until Home. Amen.

Devotion 16

EVEN WHEN OUR HOPE FAILS, HE BRINGS US BACK TO HOPEFUL

Verse: "I have said these things to you, that in me you may have peace. In the world you will have tribulation. But take heart; I have overcome the world." John 16:33

In yet another waiting room, a man caught my attention. Frail but strong somehow—towering over his cane as his kind eyes scanned the room for a seat.

When he sat down, I told him, "I love your hat."

To which he smiled with a gentle, "Thank you."

There was no mistaking what that hat covered. His frailness, sunken face, slowed gait all testified to a body ravaged by chemo and cancer.

But. His. Laugh.

The first time it pealed through the waiting room was absolute heaven. And giggling right alongside was his wife—so joyful that I almost overlooked the gray in her hair and the wrinkles on her face. They shuffled up together when the receptionist called their last name, but not before giggling, because she had certifiably butchered it.

And so I went back to reading my whatever, secretly hoping that when they were done, they would find their way back to the seats next to mine.

And when they did, I spoke to her. I can't remember what I said, only the moment we recognized one another.

She had just asked, "How old are your babies?" To which I went down the line with a "Ten, eight, six, and two."

He giggled with a raspy, "Whew." And with a playful tap she talked over him: "Two girls. Two boys. But one of my girls died when she was five years old."

I could barely breathe out an "I'm-so-sorry" before she continued. "But girl, I have hope. I have hope and joy and the promise that I will see her again."

And then, with tears in my eyes, I said, "I have hope too."

We poured out our hard. We poured out our love for Jesus. We poured out our wish for community in this sometimes whackadoo world.

A world that might only notice our differences: Our age. Our skin color. Our stories. But something bigger took its place:

Our Jesus.

Our Jesus was the same.

His love. His grace. His comfort. His unabashed faithfulness in the middle of hard things.

And y'all, even when it may seem like the world is falling down around us, this is where our hope belongs.

No matter the hard. No matter the loss. No matter the madness.

We have hope.

A hope so beautiful that it can take strangers and turn them into friends if only for a moment. A hope so bonding that when the time comes to say goodbye, you hug each other tightly as if to say, "I can't wait to see you again."

Questions: Where are you struggling to find hope in your own life? In what ways is your hurt leaving you bound to what feels hopeless? How has that changed your perception of suffering?

Prayer: Father, may we place our hope firmly in You. May we live in a way that speaks Your name. And may we release our story's outcome for the certainty of forever with You. Amen.

Devotion 17

EVEN WHEN WE SEE ONLY THE MUNDANE, HE IS DOING THE EXTRAORDINARY

Verse: "He has made everything beautiful in its time." Ecclesiastes 3:11

Some days are longer than others, some more filled with life. On one such day, one of my four kids lay in bed with pink eye, two with the flu. And by the time my husband had called on his way home from work, another kid had just announced that she *might* have had some really strange poop.

To keep the germs contained, I asked my husband if he would go in my place to deliver a little bag of love to our sweet Mimi, who was in the hospital recovering from a stroke.

About the time I finally snuggled down into bed, I heard the garage door open and knew he was home.

A part of me sighed in relief, and another part of me tried not to be a whole heap of resentful that I had done all the evening things alone.

But as he walked through the bedroom door, he quickly offered, "I'm sorry that I'm so late, but I tucked her into bed, brushed her hair, and put on Chapstick. Then we got her into her fuzzy socks, and I rearranged her pillows and blankets, so she was comfortable. And of course, I made sure her ice water was fresh."

To this I eked out a small and unimpressive, "Thank you so much, honey."

But what he didn't know is that not long after he left to go back downstairs for something, I sat in the quiet of his absence trying to fight back tears. He had loved her well because he loved me well in all the little mundane ways God has asked him to love me.

Helping me put on socks and shoes when I can't do it on my own. Brushing my hair and applying ChapStick in every hospital room I've ever been in. Rearranging my pillows and blankets every night. Bringing me ice water or chocolate or anything else I want so that I can save steps. Gently sliding my glasses off when I have fallen asleep during a movie for the millionth time.

His hands so close to the hands of my Father, bringing an offering of love so steady and sweet that it might not seem extraordinary.

Until it is.

Standing in front of me. Weathered by time. Mended by grace. Surprising me still.

Questions: Where have you been surprised by the ordinary? How might you intentionally see God in the mundane? In what ways can this pursuit spark gratitude?

Prayer: Father, may we open our eyes to the grace of the mundane, the ordinary, the everyday. May we lay down the world's expectations in exchange for the humdrum and holy. And may we forever give thanks for the gift of the little things. Amen.

Devotion 18

EVEN WHEN WE SHAKE IN ANGER, HE MEETS US AT OUR POINT OF PAIN

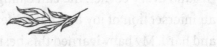

Verse: "Surely he has borne our griefs and carried our sorrows; yet we esteemed him stricken, smitten by God, and afflicted. But he was pierced for our transgressions; he was crushed for our iniquities; upon him was the chastisement that brought us peace, and with his wounds we are healed." Isaiah 53:4-5

I turned the corner into our Mimi's hospice room to find a breathtaking view: My oldest girl's lips moving gently. Her hands holding Mimi's. Her posture of absolute love as she said goodbye.

She had been denied this moment before—the chance to say goodbye—and part of me shook in anger that her twelve-year-old world had been so often ripped apart. Part of me sobbed, knowing this would change her, grow her up too quickly. And part of me stood wrecked in imagining what I feared the most:

The day she would have to say goodbye to me.

This is the bittersweet of almost-goodbyes.

Around every corner, life can change in an instant. Be it an intersection of joy and pain, life and death, or happy and hard. My baby learned this beside her Mimi's death-bed, a sacred place where we also learned we can face even the most unimaginable corners together.

Because no matter what awaits, Jesus is there, and He will not leave.

In all the noise of our suffering, we may think He's left. We may find it difficult to see His good in all our hard. We may wonder if in the middle of our hurt we will reach out and find nothing.

But I can tell you from the depths of me, the places both hard-edged and broken and soft and seeking, the voice

Devotion 19

EVEN WHEN WE FEEL DISGRACED, HE GIVES US GRACE

Verse: "But the Lord God helps me; therefore I have not been disgraced; therefore I have set my face like a flint, and I know that I shall not be put to shame." Isaiah 50:7

I had watched girl after girl walk out of church into a wind that had shown them no mercy. But bless my short-term memory and curse you, April wind. By the time church had come and gone, so had my dignity.

About halfway to our car, that wind broke loose. And when my baby girl's headband certifiably launched into the air, some kind of accessory insanity took over and I became a woman possessed.

In retrospect, I should have let the headband go. But pressing into a wind that could only be rivaled by Mary Poppins and the flyaway nannies, I kept going. Only after a near dive into the pavement did I give in, and we stumbled back to the van, with me teetering on my cane.

As we neared our Honda sanctuary, my dress was flying, and by the time I could have saved the world from a granny panty exhibition, it was too late.

As I cackled my way into the passenger seat, all the children shouted in unison, "Mom, your dress!"

"I know, I know, but the headband . . ."

Whereupon my husband began stalking the underside of every car in the parking lot until our son yelled, "It's under the truck! I've so got this, people!"

With one ninja move, this kid bounded out of the sliding car door into a face plant onto the ground only to shout, "Ugh, I can't reach it." But then as if the Holy Spirit spoke to us all at once, we yelled back in unison, "Use the cane!"

No words can describe the sight of our wind-conquering, cane-toting ninja walking back to the van with his arms raised in victory, the headband in one hand and the cane in the other. It was as he opened the door to cheers and accolades that I turned to Nathan and said, "At least no one saw this preciousness. Let us rejoice in that."

But no sooner had these words left my lips than a still small voice from the back of the van said, "The people who own that truck have been standing on the sidewalk since Mom mooned the world."

Well. Then. There it is. The utter humiliation of life and all its ridiculous ways.

Sometimes, we will mercifully face the bare-bottomed truth of our humanity without an audience. Sometimes, we will swallow our pride only before those who love us. And sometimes, we will moon the whole world.

But no matter where we find ourselves, God waits with a grace big enough for every moon-worthy moment. Be it in the laughter of our children or the kindness of a stranger or the work of the cross, His grace means we don't ever have to live in disgrace.

Questions: How does shame keep you from experiencing the fullness of His love? What pieces of your story feel beyond redemption? How can you lean into the sufficiency of His grace even in your moon-the-world moments?

Prayer: Father, may we turn to You in all that begs to bring us shame. May we hold tightly to the power of Your redemption. And may we find Your arms ready and wide open, knowing that even where the world might shame us, You stand ready to embrace us. Amen.

Devotion 20

EVEN WHEN WE MISS HIS PRESENCE, HE IS PRESENT

Verse: "You will seek me and find me, when you seek me with all your heart." Jeremiah 29:13

"Tell me a story, Mama."

Somewhere I'm sure I heard her. But I was driving, and there were errands to be done and appointments to go to and "Tell me a story, Mama!"

Somehow her eyes pierced mine through the rearview mirror. But I was parking and there were coats to put on and a boot that had fallen off and "Mama?"

Her voice was quieter now and her hands were cupped around my face, "Mama, I need you to tell me a story about Pop Pop."

And then it hit. The lump in my throat. The momentary sting in my eyes. And the complete disregard for any agenda or plan. She was here, and her Pop Pop no longer was. And she needed to remember him.

"Mama?"

"Okay, sis, OK. I'll tell you a story."

But before I could say another word, she stopped me with a "Hold on, hold on . . . I have to find him." I smiled a bit and even attended to the discarded boot until I looked up and saw her face.

She had closed her eyes.

To. Find. Him.

His face. His eyes. His scruffy beard.

All in place so that when I started my story, she *saw* him.

From there we went to that time watering flowers in the summer while he held her hand, to the two of them giving each other Eskimo kisses, to their walks in the park just a few streets down.

She laughed and smiled and remembered.

And so did I.

Later that day, I thought about my girl and her story. I thought about her eyes shut tight. And I thought about her little words, "I need to find him."

How many times had I needed the same? How many times had I needed to shut the world out? How many times had I forgotten to simply find *Him*?

When my world fell down. When my heart felt untethered. When my hard stuff dampened the joy I knew I needed.

How many times had I missed it?

The contour of His face. The love in His eyes. The grace in His countenance.

How many times had I skipped over the chance to say to the world in all its agenda and noise, "Hold on, hold on. I have to find Him."

Too. Darn. Many.

But then come days when life is a little hard-edged and uncertain. When I close my eyes and remember His mercy. When I am reminded that every day is a new day and a new chance to find Him and cry out a daughter's praise.

Questions: Where does the noise of your life drown out God's voice? How committed is your heart to finding Him even in life's commotion? How can you quell the noise and seek Him first when morning comes?

Prayer: Father, may we seek Your face in the morning, in the evening, and in every hour in-between. May we know the richness of Your faithfulness and the comfort of Your unending mercy. May we lay today's brokenness down in exchange for Your praise. Amen.

Devotion 21

EVEN WHEN WE CAN'T ALWAYS SEE IT, HE GIVES OUR PAIN PURPOSE

Verse: "Blessed be the God and Father of our Lord Jesus Christ, the Father of mercies and God of all comfort, who comforts us in all our affliction, so that we may be able to comfort those who are in any affliction, with the comfort with which we ourselves are comforted by God." 2 Corinthians 1:3-4

As I fumbled with my car keys, I saw a sweet, elderly gentleman pulling into the grocery store parking spot in front of us.

While (quite unsuccessfully) piling my own minions into our minivan, I watched as he struggled to free a cane from his car. Watched as he stopped, rested, and nearly tumbled over before making it through the double doors into the store.

And that's when I yelled at my eldest, "I'll be right back!"— leaving those in the entire parking lot to question my sanity as my girl hung out the driver's side window.

Moving as quickly as my stumbly legs would carry me, I made it through the sliding door to find he had found a cart, steadied his gait, and was slowly moving forward. So, instead of any fumbled acts of heroism, I simply offered him a smile.

When I made it back to the minivan, my girl was still hanging out the window and now yelling, "What in the world are you doing?" So I coaxed her back inside and gently explained, "Mama was just trying to make sure the man parked in front of us was OK."

"Did you ask him if he needed any help?"

I shook my head.

"Why on earth not?" she chastised.

"Because, love, when your body doesn't work like everyone else's, sometimes you just need to feel brave. You need to know you did the impossible. You need to be able to say, 'Yes, I walked through the grocery store without falling down or needing assistance.'"

And that's when my eyes began to sting. And I said something out loud I never imagined I would say, "Jesus, thank You for a stroke and a wonky left side. Thank You for fumbling feet and a mind easily confused. Thank You for every broken piece of me."

Because all of it and more had given me the ability to slip into this dear man's shoes, to understand what it meant to quietly smile in his direction, and to recognize courage in a way I would never have been able to see before.

Pain is hard. Loss is hard. Humility is hard.

But don't ever believe that pain, loss, and humility are ever without purpose. For they boldly open our eyes to the everyday courage of the very people we were meant to love.

Questions: In what way has the pain of others provided comfort in your hardest places? How has that kind act then enabled you to speak comfort over someone else? How can you move forward in gratitude toward what you struggle with now, knowing that it will likely be used in the life of another?

Prayer: Father, may we look on all that endeavors to break us as, instead, rich ground on which comfort can grow. May we hold our affliction open to those who need its common ground. And may we speak life into the hearts of those who need our comfort. Amen.

Devotion 22

EVEN WHEN WE LONG TO BE IN CONTROL, HE IS WORTHY OF OUR TRUST

Verse: "Trust in him at all times, O people; pour out your heart before him; God is a refuge for us." Psalm 62:8

Even now I remember Emily.

The soft cadence of her voice giggling out, "Miss Mang!" The hint of her shampoo spilling over her hug around my neck. The delight in her grin as she watched me discover months of missing handouts in her backpack.

You see, Emily changed me.

Not all at once, but step-by-step, inch-by-inch, giggle-by-glorious-giggle.

She was not bound by her wheelchair or her cognitive function. She did not see life for its limitation. She did not wallow in her differences. She lived and thrived and drank from a well of freedom.

But high school can be cruel, so as her teacher, I tried to protect her.

I hovered. I monopolized. I controlled.

So much so, I assigned myself as her permanent drama partner.

And then one day, someone threatened our little cocoon. A girl who was tough and brash and even a little angry. The last person in the world I would have chosen to work with Emily.

But I was caught off guard in the swirl of class starting, such that her query barely registered. "Miss Mang, I want to work with Emily today, OK?"

"Uh, er, OK . . ."

The moment I said it, I full-on panicked. So again, I ridiculously hovered. But then something beautiful happened.

I saw this angry girl smile and relax and soften. I saw Emily respond to her in a way she had never done with me. I saw growth in both of them of which I had no part, and it was breathtaking.

And we three almost missed it.

We almost missed it because of my ignorance and fear. As well-meaning as I was, I had loved Emily by trying to be all things to her, instead of trusting God to love her best.

It strikes me even now that Emily was preparing me for a journey I couldn't have imagined: motherhood, physical limitation, cognitive dysfunction. And greater still, fear.

Fear that I will not be able to be everything to my children. Fear that I might fail to protect them from the brash, angry girl in the classroom. And fear that, someday, the world will look at the result of my labor and label me as the incompetent boob I often feel like.

But shades of Emily fight my insecurity. I remember that control is more human than holy, because it's built on fear that drains us. God never meant for us to be imprisoned by our own control. Instead, He longs to set us free.

Questions: In what places of your life do you struggle with control? How does fear feed that control? Where can you begin to trust God more and fully claim the freedom He offers?

Prayer: Father, may we lay our need to control down at Your feet. May we trust in Your prevailing purpose. May we surrender our ignorance and insecurity so we may freely drink in Your freedom. Amen.

EVEN WHEN OUR PAIN TURNS THE WORLD AWAY, HE WILL STAY

Verse: "God is our refuge and strength, a very present help in trouble." Psalm 46:1

I could feel my face turning a deep red as I tried to coax my daughter out from underneath the chair.

I bargained. I affirmed. I bribed.

I pulled out every parenting *whatever* that you could possibly think of just to get her onto the exam table, including an oh so loving, "Suck it up, sister."

Finally, I cried uncle.

I turned to the nurse and said he'd need to get someone to help me lift her. I apologized all over myself. I think I even promised everyone cookies.

"It's just two shots, sister." I said dismissively.

And then the screaming began.

Screaming that grew louder and louder with every second that passed, only to crescendo into ear piercing when he returned with reinforcements.

About the time I thought about screaming too, I heard the nurse say, "Can you put your hand on her chest?" I nodded and then looked down at my girl. The moment I saw her face, any frustration and embarrassment I'd felt disappeared.

When I saw her tears, her fear, her pain, I stroked her face and said, "Look into my eyes, sister." And the very second her eyes met mine, mine began to sting.

My girl hurt. My girl was afraid. My girl felt alone. It was written all over her big brown eyes.

As I held her gaze, I could not help but think of two days earlier, when I had cried because of physical pain—something I have only done maybe three times in my life.

My girl's tears brought me to a place where I could see myself curled up on the floor begging for God to take away my hurt, feeling scared and alone.

As I drew up my hands to cradle her face, I saw a Father who grieves over my pain and draws my own face toward His. I saw His tears fall gently with mine.

No frustration. No embarrassment. No sarcastic "Suck it up, Sara."

Just a Father drawing near to a heartbroken me.

In so many ways, we seem to believe that our pain is met by a God who is standing in the corner saying, "Can you just get over this already?"

But He is not, friends.

Tears streaming down my face.

He. Is. Not.

He is present. He is near. He is standing right next to us, with His hand on our hearts, waiting for us to look deeply into His tear-filled eyes and know He will hold us through the storm and all the way Home.

Questions: Name one time you dismissed the pain of others only to later need their presence in your own pain. How has God met you in your hurt? How can you lean into the grace of knowing He is present in your pain?

Prayer: Father, may we live a life that reflects Your presence in our suffering. May we lean in deeply to the peace You offer when storms come. And may we open our hearts to the grace You sing over us even in the darkness. Amen.

Devotion 24

EVEN WHEN LOSS LEAVES US BROKEN, HE GIFTS US WITH LOVE'S LEGACY

Verse: "But you, O Lord, know me; you see me, and test my heart toward you." Jeremiah 12:3

"Mama, the flowers are here! The flowers are heeeeeere!"

My lips drew into a smile as I peeked around the corner to see daffodils. Bright, yellow, and unapologetically bold. Taking me back to the day my father came to the door with them in hand.

It was my first Mother's Day with a baby in my arms. And I recall looking skeptically at him and asking, "What am I supposed to do with those, Daddy?"

He chuckled and answered, "Well, plant them, of course."

I sighed a sigh I wish now that I hadn't, then continued with, "But really, Dad? Flowers have never been my thing. Dried out and dead is their destiny."

And yet he kept insisting, "But these come back. Every year, they will come back to remind you of your very first Mother's Day." So I laughed in disbelief and watched while he went to work.

How I wish I could have frozen that moment in time. The dirt beneath his fingernails. The sweat wiped away with a white handkerchief. The sweet way his glasses would slip down to the tip of his nose.

How. I. Wish.

But time passed, the flowers came and went again and again and again, and then in a blink, he was gone.

I had almost forgotten about them until a few days before my first birthday without him.

The sun was scorching and the kids were bored, so I wrangled our very lame sprinkler to the backyard in hopes it would stop the whining. Frankly, I would have been psyched at a mere thirty minutes of happiness if only for the chance to go to the bathroom uninterrupted. Because, sweet heavens, the struggle is just so very real.

But as I walked back to the front yard, something yellow caught my eye.

My daddy's daffodils.

Bright, beautiful, and so unapologetically bold that I could do nothing but smile. It was as though in all the madness and the tangled emotions of my loss, he was saying, "I'm here, Sara Bear. I'm here."

But there on our doorstep my heart realized something it already knew: my parents' anniversary was *on* my birthday. So these flowers were meant for someone else entirely.

My *mama*.

I watered and watched and made sure that when the fourteenth came, the daffodils were arranged and cut in a vase my daddy had given me, topped off with a card that said, "Flowers from your love."

And every year since, they've bloomed just in time.

We all watch and wait and wonder together until the day when someone comes running in the front door and shouts, "The flowers are here, Mama! The flowers are heeeeeere!"

I still clip and cut and arrange them in the same sweet vase so that on the fourteenth of June we can show up at Mama's door with flowers from my dad. And my heart can't help but smile every year at the absolute delight in her voice as she exclaims, "When you said you were coming, I was hoping this is what you'd bring!"

Maybe that is the gift of loss. You see love differently. You marvel at its simplicity. You give more of who you are in every day. So that when you are gone, your love can stay.

That love may be quiet or unexpected or unapologetically bold. But no matter how it comes, such a rooted thing cannot help but reach through the madness of life and say, "I'm here."

Questions: Where have you found His love even in your pain? What kind of legacy of love has been written on your own heart? How can you extend that legacy to others?

Prayer: Father, may we see the beauty of Your love in unexpected ways. May we embrace the ashes and the pain, knowing You will bring beauty from them. And when our lives draw to a close, may it be said of us we left behind a legacy of love. Amen.

Devotion 25

EVEN WHEN STORMS TRY TO OVERTAKE US, HE MAKES US BRAVE

Verse: "Be strong and courageous. Do not be frightened, and do not be dismayed, for the Lord your God is with you wherever you go." Joshua 1:9

Six weeks before my fortieth birthday, my son grew obsessed over the idea of taking me to Build-A-Bear. He posted reminder notes, added caveats to bedtime prayers, and even scribbled an addition to our summer bucket list.

Now I would like to say I paid attention. Or that I asked him why. Or that I had mama intuition out the yin-yang.

But that would be a big fat lie.

Instead, I pushed off and set aside and ignored. I was busy. I was tired. I was whatever I was at the moment. And life just seemed bigger than my boy's slight obsession.

Until one night when my eldest girl came into my bedroom, snuggled up to me, and said, "Mom, do you know why he wants you to go to Build-A-Bear? He knows another surgery is coming up, and he doesn't want you to be alone at the hospital. He thought a bear with our kisses inside would help you to be brave."

My heart fell as I half-whispered, "Really?"

She nodded back and said, "I just thought you should know."

So I brushed a few tears away and grew determined to find the greatest of bears so my boy knew I was cared for and loved while out of his reach.

The next day, he held my hand tightly as we entered the store, letting go only to grab the perfect bear and carry it around from station to station with his sisters in tow— kissing hearts, settling on an outfit, choosing a name. Eventually he told me: "Meet Dr. Snuggles."

On our walk back to the car, I realized I *was* braver somehow.

Braver because a little boy had seen my struggle and had determined to walk me through it. Braver because his love broke through the noise of a busy life—leaving me to remember that bravery is not a thing that comes from your own strength.

Bravery instead comes from the love that walks with you.

Be it from a Father who will carry you on the days you cannot carry yourself. Or a friend who shows up ready to join you in the messiest messes. Or a little boy whose heart only knows that a bear had once made him feel brave.

Love will shout and scribble and show up. If only to walk us all the way to the hard places we must go. Knowing that, in the end, we will all be a little bit braver somehow.

Questions: When have you had to borrow someone else's brave? In what ways has that breathed grace into your own pain? Moving forward, how can you break through the noise of your life to hear the needs of others?

Prayer: Father, may we stand ready to welcome the courage and blessing of another. May we see their care as a gift from You. And may we see the grace of those willing to walk into our messes and show up even at our protest. Amen.

Devotion 26

EVEN WHEN ALL SEEMS LOST, HE SHOWS US THE WAY HOME

Verse: "For this light momentary affliction is preparing for us an eternal weight of glory beyond all comparison." 2 Corinthians 4:17

I remember the day I knew that my Mimi was somehow changed. Knew she had moved beyond forgetful. Knew her life was fading into the recesses of her brilliant but dementia-riddled mind.

I remember the hum of the breathing machine. Her breath moving with a steady in and out. Her eye roll and indignation that such a thing would interrupt our chat. Her sweet little hand reaching for mine as if to say, "Don't go."

But as it always does, life beckoned me home and I had to say our usual goodbye.

A squish. A kiss. A whole mess of "I love yous." And yet?

Something in the usual seemed changed.

It started the minute I began to gather my things and she asked, "Is it OK if I sit in the front seat?" To which I turned and smiled and chalked it up to a little post-stroke confusion. But as I bent down to hug her, she started to stand as though a wheelchair no longer seemed necessary.

So I sat her down gently with, "Oh, Mimi, you have to stay here. Remember, you are in the hospital, and we are trying to get you better so you can be home with Papa?"

But she started to stand again, insisting, "I want to go home with you. I want to sit in the front seat. I promise we'll have fun and I'll be good."

Tears began to well in my eyes as I pressed our foreheads together, sat her down, and said, "Mimi, I want nothing more than to bring you home with me right this second. But you still have some important work to do here."

Her eyes grew wide, and tears began to fall as she whispered, "Well, that is just the pits." And I had to agree, "Yes, it is, sweet girl. Yes, it is. But I promise: home is coming soon."

Two months later, I would see those wide, tear-filled eyes again.

Longing for her husband, searching his face for the last time, draping her tiny body over his coffin, saying again what her words could not, "I want to go Home with you."

Yet something in her stayed a few months longer, and I cannot help but think it was love.

Love for her girl who had lost so much. Love for her grandbabies and great grandbabies whose hearts needed a chance to say goodbye. Love for her boy who needed to be there when she finally went Home.

And now? All that was taken from her has been restored. Giving way to a hope that softly pulls me forward.

Forward toward a sweet promise so familiar I can almost hear her calling:

"Soon, Sara. Home is coming soon."

Questions: When has pain held you captive? Where have others shown you the hope of what's waiting? How can you see past your pain to the grace of forever?

Prayer: Father, may we offer our heartbreak and pain as an opportunity to know You more. May we let go of the temporal, the fleeting, the fly-by-night hope this world offers. And may we exchange it for the promise of a forever Home with You. Amen.

EVEN WHEN WE FORGET WHO WE ARE, HE REMINDS US WHOSE WE ARE

Verse: "I stretch out my hands to you; my soul thirsts for you like a parched land." Psalm 143:6

My heart felt lighter the moment I saw the man with the smiling eyes and dapper button-down. He moved steadily toward me down the hallway of memory care, his walker donning a bright-red homemade valentine.

It seemed such a strange juxtaposition to the loss of my Mimi the day before, so I stopped and said with all the cheer I had in me, "I love your Valentine."

A half-smile crept across his face with only a hint of confusion.

He stood there for a moment reveling in my compliment, and then he became serious, his tone hushed and his hand now squarely on my shoulder: "I need to go to that one place, so I can go somewhere. But I'm not sure where. It's at the one place down that way there."

Round and round he'd go, trying to tell me he desperately wanted to find someone or something.

As his confusion and nervousness grew, I leaned in to say, "Well, you know, I think I've been there. So why don't we try to find it together?"

His eyes softened and his breathing slowed as we made our way to the front of memory care.

As we turned the corner toward the community room, I noticed a beautiful woman with silver hair approaching us. His walker slowed a bit at the sight of her. It was as though he recognized something and yet couldn't be sure of who she was until she said, "Hey, you."

His eyes filled with tears as he turned to me and said, "It's her!"

And I could do no more than answer back, "You did it! You found her."

Even without a name, his heart knew who he had been looking for—the one his soul loved—even though his mind had the audacity to stand in his way.

Feeling a little intrusive in that sacred moment, I walked away with something deeply pressed into my heart.

Our bodies, our minds, our memories are meant to fade, but even in the fading, there is something that stays. A longing for the One our hearts love most.

No person can take Him from us. No disease can take Him from us. No circumstance can take Him from us.

We are His and He is ours, forever and always.

Questions: In what ways do you seek God even in weakness? Where can you surrender your mind and body to the mercy of knowing your heart will always be His? How can you begin to live within that promise?

Prayer: Father, may our hands stretch upward. May our eyes seek Your face. And may our hearts always remember even when our minds cannot that nothing can take You or Your hand from us. Amen.

Devotion 28

EVEN WHEN WE DOUBT HIS FAITHFULNESS, HE REMAINS FAITHFUL

Verse: "Then Samuel took a stone and set it up between Mizpah and Shen and called its name Ebenezer; for he said, 'Till now the Lord has helped us.'" I Samuel 7:12

Sometimes life can sucker punch us in the best way possible.

Stealing our breath. Grabbing our attention. Forcing us to remember the hard things of our past so we can rest in knowing God will be there in the present.

Such was one evening visit to the ER.

After a seven-night, no-sleep marathon, I had finally cried uncle and let my hubs drop me off for a shot of steroids and pain meds—a little cavalier in our attitude about this place we frequented almost as much as the grocery store. We even gave each other an air high-five as he headed home, and I made my way through the double doors.

Despite my sleep-deprived fugue state, I recognized something familiar about the nurse doing my intake.

I wrestled with it as she took down my name, checked off all the drugs, and updated my chart. But then she asked the question that even now makes me cringe because I know what question usually follows: "I see here you have gone into respiratory arrest. Is that part of the autoimmune disease?"

So I grudgingly answered back, "No. I came into the ER in shock from sepsis."

"And what caused that?"

As it so happens, this question always makes me stare at my feet. I mustered up a mercifully quick answer, "Miscarriage. I had an incomplete miscarriage."

What happened next stole my breath, because when I looked up, I saw tears streaming down her face. "Oh, Sara. I thought it was you. I was there that day. We were all so scared you weren't going to make it. . . ."

She had been the nurse on duty when, years earlier, I had crawled through the same double doors with a 107-degree temperature and my body in septic shock. The staff had fought for hours to stabilize me enough for transport so doctors could operate. Even after surgery, I woke up on a ventilator in the ICU.

Person after person called my survival a miracle.

And so I thanked this nurse the best way I knew how. I told her all about our rainbow baby. I showed her pictures of the family we'd become. And then I hugged her closely and softly whispered, "Thank you for not giving up on me. The life you gave back to me is such a beautiful one."

God writes miracles across the landscape of our lives— some seem hard-edged, a juxtaposition of beauty and loss. Others tuck themselves into simple, mundane moments of our everyday. But no matter where they grow, they remind us He is active in the details. One moment, one day, one miracle at a time.

Questions: What miracles has He wrought in your own life? How might those miracles be raised as a testimony of His faithfulness? How can you offer that testimony to others?

Prayer: Father, may we raise up Your faithfulness in our lives as an Ebenezer, a stone of help in our darkest moments. May we remember that You are faithful to help us even when we are helpless. And may we trust You with our tomorrows, knowing who You have been in our yesterdays. Amen.

Devotion 29

EVEN WHEN WE FACE OUR GREATEST STRUGGLE, HE DOES NOT LEAVE US ALONE IN OUR PAIN

Verse: "You have kept count of my tossings; put my tears in your bottle. Are they not in your book?" Psalm 56:8

My daughter's eyes broke me. Brimming with tears. Holding hurt in every blink.

I cupped her face and pressed my forehead against hers and whispered, "I'm so sorry, love. But I'm right here and I will carry this with you."

Test after test. Appointment after appointment. Poke after poke.

We came to find a tender understanding of one another in this place—a place of fear and uncertainty that brought both tears and laughter. A place where light and love could coexist with suffering and pain. Tucked in-between all that is bittersweet and sacred and known by a name all too familiar.

Chronic illness.

I had walked nearly twenty years in its wake. But this was different. Harder. More tender. Because this was my baby.

So I found myself wrestling with fear and anger and the in-between of guilt and grief. The doubt of all I should have done swirling around in my mama's heart. A battle that felt too big to fight.

But somewhere in the middle of all its ugliness, we have found each other.

In early morning car trips to the hospital. In the counting and care of the mother and daughter pillboxes. In

the see-you-soon hugs before she's wheeled off to a pro-
cedure room. In the moments where her tears stop and
mine somehow begin.

Me and my girl holding onto hope together.

It is not the road I would have chosen, but it is every bit
the destination:

A place of shared understanding from the hands and
heart of someone who has walked a similar road. In this
place, we see Jesus a little more clearly, if we only dare
humble ourselves to invite others into our suffering.

Because in suffering we can tangibly feel Him bend
down, hands to our faces, forehead to forehead, if only
to whisper, "I'm so sorry, love. But I'm right here and
I will carry this with you."

Questions: Where have you found God's beauty in
a shared struggle? In what ways have you seen that
beauty grow with time? How has He used your tearstained moments to speak into the tearstained moments
of others?

Prayer: Father, may we find rest in knowing that our pain is measured in purpose. May we have the courage to invite others into our suffering without condition or hesitation. And may we find comfort in knowing that, if we are so brave, You will never leave us alone in the struggle. Amen.

Devotion 30

EVEN WHEN THE DARKNESS OF NIGHT SURROUNDS US, HE COMFORTS US

Verse: "God is in the midst of her; she shall not be moved; God will help her when morning dawns." Psalm 46:5

"I fink I had a bad dream," my six-year-old whispered, with her nose pressed right to mine. Her sweet little hand touching my face as I turned to find it was only four in the morning.

Tired me wanted to say, "Go back to bed, sister." Selfish me wanted to pretend I was still sleeping.

But then something in me paused and went back to the day before.

A conversation. A Zoom call. A kindergarten class.

Little faces on the screen and one amazing teacher trying her best to make it all feel somewhat normal—with me as the remote learning helper. Starting every morning with a little conversation starter to break the kindergarten ice.

A prompt. A story. A question.

On this particular morning, every tiny voice answered, "What makes you feel loved?"

I was ready for the hilarious answers:

"I feel loved when my mom gives me five popsicles."

(Because, really, are four popsicles ever enough?)

"Cold hard cash."

(Can you even stand it?)

What I wasn't prepared for was getting a little misty at the simplicity of their answers:

"A kiss from my mommy."

"A hug goodnight from my daddy."

"A bike ride with my family."

"A cookie I eat with my grandma."

Nothing fancy, nothing over-the-top, nothing extravagant, nothing that required much (save the cold hard cash), but each answer held one thing in common: the presence of someone who loved them.

As their answers came to an end, the little one next to me leaned over to whisper in my ear, "Mom, I know I already said mine, but I have another one—I also feel loved when you hold me after a bad dream."

So, what was I to do at four o'clock the next morning but take her hand, lift her into my bed, and do what God has done for me a thousand nights before?

Draw her close, hold her tightly, and stay with her until the sun came up.

Bringing us both to the heart of the One who holds us and helps us meet whatever comes. Be it exhaustion or fear over life's biggest nightmares, He is and always will be ready to carry and comfort us all the way to morning's dawn.

Questions: Where has God's love found you in the darkness of the night? In what ways has it made you feel known? How can you show His transformational love to someone else?

Prayer: Father, may we find You in the middle of our darkest nights. May we speak into the void knowing that You hold us, love us, cherish us. And may we dwell deeply in Your loving care, knowing that morning is coming with mercy anew. Amen.

EVEN WHEN WE HAVE SO VERY LITTLE TO OFFER, HE STILL CHOOSES US

Verse: "For God so loved the world, that he gave his only Son, that whoever believes in him should not perish but have eternal life." John 3:16

We are a messy Easter crew.

Beyond ill-fated dresses and over-the-top shenanigans, I often wonder if we are messy because God moves toward us with such abject care that we cannot help but be undone.

Such was Holy week one year, when we had poop on the floor and Sharpie on the wall. When we wailed and dropped things and lost our minds. When we could not hold it together if our lives had depended on it. We were so incredibly messy it hurt.

And then Good Friday came, and I could not help but feel the weight of all that had rained down.

The kids were piling out of the van covered in powdered sugar from our donut "brunch." And I just needed a moment. So I shut the sliding doors, turned to a grown-up Jesus song, and closed my eyes.

Just for a moment . . .

But then a little voice came from the back seat, "You OK, Mama?"

It was only then I realized I was sobbing uncontrollably. Sobbing even as I tried to answer back. Sobbing because in that strange little moment of peace, my smelly, messy minivan had become my Gethsemane.

Somewhere my heart knew to answer back, "No, I'm not, baby but I'm gonna be."

The truth was, I felt lost in all the ways a mama can. Trying to reconcile a counter full of sippy cups alongside pillboxes and doctor's notes. Taking family pictures with matching outfits and smiling faces after spending the afternoon talking trauma and suicidal ideation with my baby's counselor. Being lauded in public for loving my babies while knowing all the while that I was failing in private.

We've all felt the dissonance. And we can either stay stuck there, or we can embrace the only way forward: scraping and clawing toward the truth that *God chose us.*

He chose our hard and our messy and our broken. He chose us even knowing that we would doubt and wrestle and flail.

And this can wreck us in the best way possible. Leading us to freely say, even amid tears: "It may not be OK, but I know I'm gonna be."

Questions: Where has life threatened to beat you down? In what ways do you feel dissonance in your life right now? How does the knowledge that God has chosen you relieve some of the weight you carry?

Prayer: Father, may we find You under every hurt we carry. May we seek Your face when the pain feels too heavy to bear alone. And may we remember the choice Jesus made so we could have the hope of forever with You. Amen.

Devotion 32

EVEN WHEN LIFE IS CRUEL, HE ASKS US TO BE KIND

Verse: "Therefore, as God's chosen people, holy and dearly loved, clothe yourselves with compassion, kindness, humility, gentleness and patience." Colossians 3:12 NIV

I recognized the sweet voice on the drive-through intercom even though I was simultaneously scrounging around for change, smoothing my bedhead, and wondering if I had even brushed my teeth.

But the woman's sweet lilt was so unmistakable, my head popped up from the scrounging with an, "Oh, sister, how are you?"

Which led to a quick interchange:

"Feeling better."

"I am sooooo glad."

"I think I'll even make it through my whole shift today! I had to go home early the day you saw me."

"I'm so grateful you did. I was worried about you."

And then with a "See ya soon!" I resumed my scrounging.

When I pulled up to the window and she handed me a cup of sweet coffee heaven, I tried to give her my minivan jackpot. But she smiled and said, "It's on me today."

Normally, I would have offered to pay for the next one in line, but all I could do was say a quiet thanks and drive away.

Not two minutes and a sip later, I felt hot tears rolling down my cheek. What does it say about this world if my simple concern for someone at the drive-through window would warm her heart so deeply that she would extend such beautiful kindness to me?

The truth is, I could see past her tough cookie act a few days earlier and noticed the effect of illness on her face because I see it in the mirror every day.

That's why, within seconds of looking at her, I had asked, "Are you OK?" And I was so proud of her for responding, "Not really. I had influenza, and even though I'm not contagious anymore, it just really wiped me out. But I need to work after missing ten days."

So I'd listened and shook my head in agreement but parted with, "Please go home if you need to." And her tired eyes had smiled back even as she nodded in response.

Kindness and compassion simply come more readily when you have already walked through someone else's kind of pain. For me, that kindness has always felt more human than heroic. And it made me wonder how many other people's pain I've missed in my rummaging-for-whatever-I-think-I-need little life.

In today's world, kindness is not simple. No, it's an intentional act of relentless love that can breathe life into the heart of another, who can then turn around and say, "It's on me today."

Questions: Where has God used your hard things to allow you to love others well? When has time kept you from loving well? How can you set time aside for the pursuit of love today?

Prayer: Father, may we open our eyes to the hurt and hard stuff of others. May we carry Your love to those the world may deem unlovely. And may we lay down our schedules, our to-do-lists, our control for the sake of Your kindness and care. Amen.

EVEN WHEN WE FACE OUR GREATEST INDIGNITY, HE GIVES US A REASON TO REJOICE

Verse: "Rejoice always, pray without ceasing, give thanks in all circumstances; for this is the will of God in Christ Jesus for you." I Thessalonians 5:16-18

Some days, you just have to thank God for wet pants.

Picture this:

A grown woman ventures out one night to a popular eatery with two friends she adores. The evening is filled with laughter, great conversation, and Godiva chocolate. The perfect respite for an otherwise crazy week.

Perfect, that is, until she stands up and realizes she has wet pants. Now keep in mind, these are not the kind of wet pants that come from a careless tip of the water glass. These are the kind of wet pants we pray our three-year-old avoids when we have mistakenly chosen the big girl panties for a two-hour road trip.

Those kind of wet pants.

Does she panic? No.

Instead, she is puzzled. "Did, I, Sara Cormany, really just wet my pants? And here, of all places?" And then the inner monologue begins: "Woman, you just wet your pants, does it matter where?"

Grateful that she is with two friends who love her, albeit befuddled, she leaves with her head held high. In the swirl of it all, she forgets if she told management that a once-over with the all-purpose cleaner might be a good idea for booth number five.

Now, why, may you ask, am I thanking God for wet pants? Why, even when my body is crazy, unpredictable, and falling apart? The answer is surprisingly simple.

Each day crazy, unpredictable things happen—so I am grateful for the 364 days that I did not have wet pants. The days I did not fumble, fall, or feel fatigued.

Grateful that I have such kind, tenderhearted friends who make me feel normal. Grateful that my God has given me a body that works most of the time. Grateful for all the ways He blesses me when life doesn't go as planned. And, most of all, grateful for a reason to smile on even the hardest of days.

So, there it is. Gratitude and a wet pair of pants. Now, of course, you might understandably ask, "*Where* is booth number five?" That, my friends, shall remain a mystery.

After all, a girl has to have some secrets.

Questions: How have life's unpredictable moments left your heart struggling with ingratitude? Looking back now, how has God met you even in those moments? Where can you embrace the grace of a newfound perspective?

Prayer: Father, may we give thanks for the crazy, the unexpected, the hilarious. May we see Your goodness in those who come alongside us in our messiness. And may we stand up to anything or anyone who might steal it away. Amen.

Devotion 34

EVEN WHEN OTHERS OVERLOOK US, HE WILL CHOOSE US

Verse: "Let us then with confidence draw near to the throne of grace, that we may receive mercy and find grace to help in time of need." Hebrews 4:16

Something about spring begs me to stop.

Perhaps it is the new life, the green against the gray, the promise held in its beauty. But sometimes I wonder if it is more about my daddy.

His love of growing things. His tending to any flower beyond hope. His watering of all that is parched.

While some might guess my daddy was a gardener, he was not so much that as he was a healer. He would walk past the beautiful, the full, the most expensive plant in the store and find the one no one wanted, the one no one saw, the one no one expected to be taken home. And he would claim it as his own.

Rolling up his sleeves and bending toward its need for him, he would begin the work of revival.

He did not turn away at a plant's appearance. He did not balk at the time it took to bring it back to life. He did not force it to bend to his agenda. Instead, he offered patience and lovingkindness in the hope of bringing about growth and green.

Something in the remembrance of my daddy's ritual rends me to my core in a world where we seem firmly planted on perfect and polished and life born from normalcy. Where we beg others to fit our schedule, our agenda, our level of comfort. Where we cluck and pick at one another's differences.

But what if we walked purposefully past put-together to find the lost, the unseen, the unwanted? What if we allowed pain to grow us, change us, bend us closer to the work of the cross? What if we traded our pursuit of the perfect life and exchanged it for the promise of a perfect forever?

What if we took time to become a healer? Tending to what's broken. Watering what's parched. And finding in others what was worth the cross.

Questions: In what way do you feel the world has overlooked you? When has God used others to remind you of your worth? How can you embrace this grace moving forward?

Prayer: Father, may we see the cracks and crevices in others as a reminder of our own humanity. May we see beauty in one another's imperfection. And may we look past appearance to find the perfect residence for Your grace. Amen.

Devotion 35

EVEN WHEN WE ARE WEARY, HE RENEWS OUR STRENGTH

Verse: "He gives power to the faint, and to him who has no might he increases strength." Isaiah 40:29

The words hung over my friend's bed in scripted letters: "Whom the Lord calls, He will use." Her smile lit up the room with her unmistakable brand of joy, yet her eyes looked weary.

She was no stranger to pain or to a body that struggles.

As a little girl, she had fought two types of polio that left her body permanently weakened. Yet God would grow her into a fierce warrior. Called to the mission field at just twelve years old, she persevered, knowing that His strength grows best in weakness. She eventually served the Kimyal tribe in Irian Jaya for nearly twenty years.

Yet on this particular occasion, drawing a deep breath, she began to say, "Some days, it's hard to be a warrior..."

My heart caught a bit in my throat as I heard and imagined the pain she described. A body fading. A heart weary. A bigger physical battle looming.

She knew what the progression of post-polio syndrome meant and stood ready to face it, but at that moment, she needed the grace to lament. So we sat in her tears and cried over her broken heart. We did so knowing the grace of a good God but also the reality of the pain this world holds.

There may be nothing more courageous than to fight a battle no one else sees.

To fight knowing the depth of struggle coming. To fight breath by breath, moment by moment, at the feet of Jesus—a place where strength and weariness can coexist.

Only here will we find courage in fear, gain in loss, and beauty in pain as they are held by a life surrendered to the truth, "Whom the Lord calls, He will use."

Questions: When has weariness brought you to the feet of Jesus? Has your weary heart ever kept you from saying yes to His calling? How can you move forward knowing that, even in weariness, He offers you strength?

Prayer: Father, may we see our weariness as the perfect ground on which strength grows. May we find a way to embrace that we are less so You can be made more. And may we fade into You so deeply that the world truly sees You in us. Amen.

Devotion 36

EVEN WHEN WE HAVE NO FIGHT LEFT IN US, HE FIGHTS FOR US

Verse: "The Lord will fight for you, and you have only to be silent." Exodus 14:14

Something familiar caught in my throat—a memory wrapped in ambulance lights and sliding doors. A place we'd been before.

Saying goodbye to my sweet daddy. Finding my Mimi lost in her own mind. Finding my ridiculous self here so many times we may as well have had a punch card.

But this time, my husband was the patient, and I was the one holding it all together on the other side.

I stood in a hospital lobby with a silly blanket covered in all things Valentine, my paltry offering for my sweet guy as he struggled for breath upstairs in the quarantined COVID-19 unit. As I gave it to the woman behind the desk, I choked out the words, "Room 788."

Then I went home to find the will and the power of what-evers. I walked both of us through the motions over the phone. I listened outside my babies' bedroom doors as he said just-in-case goodbyes.

And then I whispered my own eked-out prayers and wrestled through the night's unforgiving solitude.

This was not what we expected.

Him in the ICU fighting COVID-19. Me carrying all that came in-between.

For nine days, we made the most of hospital lobby drop-offs and homemade cards and just-in-case phone calls. While nights held tearstained prayers and holding onto Jesus, I found myself weighing the possibility of life without him and putting on my big girl pants when I'd rather dissolve into a puddle on the floor.

Until we were given a miracle and he walked back through those sliding doors and into my arms.

In the days following his release, love felt different somehow. Because I now understood the love my husband had so often carried and so steadily offered, a love that fought for me and fought for our family. Year after year. Hospitalization after hospitalization. Complication after complication.

But someone else had been fighting for us too.

God had gone before us, filling in the gaps brought by sheer exhaustion and trauma and our own brokenness. And He stands ready to do the same in every storm or stronghold we face. Reaching into the helpless places of our lives and reminding us that He will fight for us even when all we can do is be still.

Questions: When has life left you feeling helpless? When has fear prevented you from trusting God with the outcome? How can you keep your eyes on Him even in your fear?

Prayer: Father, may we seek You in the moments we feel gut-punched and bottomed out. May we trust You with the battle. And may we move forward in faith believing You will be enough in the darkest places, the deepest valleys, and our greatest fears. Amen.

Devotion 37

EVEN WHEN WE PRAY RIDICULOUS PRAYERS, HE HEARS THE CRY OF OUR HEARTS

Verse: "When the righteous cry for help, the Lord hears and delivers them out of all their troubles." Psalm 34:17

Something in my daughter's words caught my attention: "You don't have to come . . ." she said. ". . . but I need you to."

Maybe it was the number of times she said it. Maybe it was just a mama's intuition.

But whatever the maybe, her words found me barely recovered from COVID-19, hair wild and perhaps only slightly clean, driving in our minivan through western Kansas to the state speech championship.

Much like most of my spur-of-the-moment mama moves, I had not thought much through. But nowhere was this more glaring than forgetting that a girl could have a really hard time finding gas after Topeka. Especially when her gas light turns on only a hot minute from that exit.

There I was, sweating profusely sans AC to save on gas and praying a ridiculous prayer: "Jesus, please just get me some gas." I pleaded these words over and over again, while at some point wondering if I needed to specify what *kind* of gas.

After a solid forty minutes of nothing on the horizon, I upped the ante: "Jesus, please don't let this be a disaster. Please let me just be a normal mom who shows up for her kid, instead of a hot mess who ends up stranded among miles and miles of prairieland."

Then, rising out of a great expanse of nothingness, the right kind of gas appeared. And just like that, my ridiculous prayer was answered, and I showed up in time to see my girl make it to finals.

As we rolled home, gas tank and heart full, I smiled at the sight of my teen baby sleeping in the seat next to mine. And I remembered, yet again, that loving others is messy. It can gut us and wrench our hearts a million and one ways. It can test us and stretch us and show us what unconditional love really costs. But at the end of the day, it's the showing up that matters, not how pretty it looks getting there.

And for the moments where we feel lost and alone and a half a million miles from nowhere, He will be there in the chaos, bending near to hear the deepest cry of our hearts.

Breath by breath. Word by word. Prayer by ridiculous prayer.

Questions: In what ways do you feel your circumstances are beyond God's capability in your own life? Where can you lean into His strength even when you feel ill-equipped? How can this change the way you pray?

Prayer: Father, may we never forget to lift both our joy and our pain to You. May we come to Your throne with confidence that even the most outrageous request is near to Your heart. And may we lay our burden, our fears, our failures down and exchange them for the grace of Your goodness. Amen.

Devotion 38

EVEN WHEN WE FEEL BOUND TO OUR BROKENNESS, HE SETS US FREE

Verse: "Everyone who believes in him will not be put to shame." Romans 10:11

I often wonder how many people I miss in my rushing, my tasking, my reconciling of this hurried life.

But on this particular day, Jesus gave me the grace to see someone I likely would have missed.

She was sitting alone at a concert beside my husband and me, watching our failed attempts at selfie-taking to commemorate my birthday. I remember trying to decide if I should say something, hearing my teenager audibly in my head, "Mom, don't be creepy."

So at first, I started with small talk, trying to keep my creep factor to a minimum. But somewhere in the small, something big happened.

She told us about her life. She told us about her faith. She even told us about her adventure to this Tuesday-night concert (where she found herself sitting beside some inept old people who could not take a selfie to save their souls).

During the intermission, she offered to help us in our sad selfie-quest, only further convincing us she was just about the dearest girl on earth.

As the evening drew to a close and we were saying our goodbyes, I felt something in me wanting to say, "I have no doubt you make God smile every day just by being you." And so I did.

Suddenly, she was crying and hugging me tightly as she whispered through her tears. "You don't know how much that means. I've done so many things wrong.

But three months ago, I knew I needed to make it right with Him."

And somehow through my own tears I said words my own heart often failed to hear: "You didn't have to, love. Jesus already did that for you."

His love doesn't require us to be all cleaned up before we get to be worthy of it. His love doesn't say, "We need to fix you before we can sit with you." His love doesn't set out a laundry list of wrongs that we must somehow overcome.

So we must endeavor to love differently, holding onto the truth that God's love shows up, reaches out, and lays comfort down. Because He loved us first and showed us how.

Questions: Where do you struggle with the weight of your past mistakes? In what ways can you release that shame? How can you move forward in freedom?

Prayer: Father, may we trust You to bring us back to Your heart when we turn away and stray. May we lean into sufficiency of the cross in all we do. And may we walk freely in the truth that the battle is done and Your love has won. Amen.

Devotion 39

EVEN WHEN OUR DAYS DRAW TO A CLOSE, HE SHOWS US HOW TO LIVE THEM WELL

Verse: "Teach us to number our days that we may get a heart of wisdom." Psalm 90:12

Even now, my friend's words wash over me with an unencumbered grace: "I have lived very well and now I shall die well."

Diagnosed with cancer and given only weeks to live, this beloved member of our writing community offered this simple response to her terminal diagnosis in a way only she could. With humility, gentleness, and eternity in view.

From the moment we met, I watched her delight in all that life had to offer. Be it in her babies, grandbabies, or beloved husband. Be it in the writers she mentored or the colleagues she loved. Be it in the readers for whom she wrote or the elderly she served at her local nursing home.

She was always the first to send a note of congratulations for good news or a note of encouragement when life got hard. And she offered each with the same kindness and delight with which she approached life.

While her fade into eternity was brutally fast and especially heartbreaking to those closest to her, she lived up to the cry of her heart. She died as she had lived. And in offering up even her pain to us, we all learned something indelibly profound:

To die well, we must live well too.

We cannot get so bogged down in the minutia of our days or our suffering that we miss the reason we're here: to embrace the time we've been given.

This time is a gift we only discover if we are willing to surrender to it fully and freely. A gift we often find lined in pain and brokenness. A gift we might balk at until it's all we have left.

But this dear soul understood that we were never meant to work out our own good or even our own brand of a good life. Instead, we've been called to count our days so we may live out God's purpose for our lives with wisdom, embracing the truth that eternity often needs our hard stuff more than it needs our happiness.

And yet even here, He gives us the grace to choose.

To stand in the gap between here and heaven. To hold all we love with open hands. To present our days as a sacred offering.

So that when the time comes, we can say with resolved surrender, "I have lived very well and now I shall die well."

Questions: Where do you struggle to live well? Where do you wrestle with your own mortality? How do you want others to see your life against the backdrop of eternity?

Prayer: Father, may we live well, love well, serve well. May we offer up our lives as a living sacrifice. And may we face eternity with courage and a heart that longs to bring you one last best offering. Amen.

Devotion 40

EVEN WHEN WE FEEL LIKE GIVING UP, HE OFFERS US THE STRENGTH TO PRESS FORWARD

Verse: "I have fought the good fight, I have finished the race, I have kept the faith." 2 Timothy 4:7

As I crossed the stage for the first time in forever, I found my precious friend waiting for me. This gift of a woman had loved me enough to kick me into my big girl pants and fully embrace the grace of a rewritten life.

To see her standing there, waiting to celebrate with me, meant more than the award in my hands. Her arms opened and she hugged me tightly, saying, "I'm so glad you didn't give up."

I wobbled back to my seat with her words still hanging in the air, realizing something important: all too often we only see the on-stage moments. The honor. The applause. The joy. The mountain tops.

But the truth is, life is spent largely in the wings. Surrendering dreams and embracing grace.

Instead of the spotlight, we've known hospital beds and gravesides. Instead of mountaintops, we've found valleys full of things unsaid. Instead of applause, we've stood in the wake of tear-covered prayers whispered over all things tenuous and lost.

But even in the mess and the madness, we can find a beauty greater than any spotlight or applause—a milestone we never thought we'd see, a prayer answered, or a joy made full. Each takes us back to the heart of the Father who has perfectly held us, loved us, and carried us.

A Father who brings beauty from our ashes. Speaks healing through our brokenness. Breathes peace into our chaos. Weaves strength into our weakness. Brings light into our darkness. Offers freedom from our shame. And gives hope rooted in the grace of forever.

Even when we need help to make it to the other side. Even when our weakness is displayed in all its glory.

Even then, He draws us close and whispers, "I'm so glad you didn't give up."

Questions: Where has your joy been stolen by the hard things of life? How can you move forward in God's grace and begin to reclaim that joy? How can you use your hard things to testify as a part of that reclamation?

Prayer: Father, may we trust You with our story even when we cannot see the grace and good You promise. May we embrace the beauty of life's brokenness even when we cannot understand its pain. And may we live within the strength of Your love, even when the world might struggle to understand it. Even when, may we. Amen.

CONCLUSION

"If God has made your cup sweet, then drink it with grace. If he has made it bitter, drink it in communion with Him." Oswald Chambers

As I sit here readying my heart to give you one final offering, one final piece of grace, I will freely admit that my loved ones and I find ourselves in yet another season of hard things. It is a stretch of time when our hearts yearn for Home and the tender mercy only Jesus provides.

I say this only to authentically admit we are not masters of grace—we are simply receivers. We are continually learning, continually growing, continually stretching toward knowing Him more.

Even when we fail.
Even when we rage.
Even when we question.
Even when we faceplant on the floor.

It is in this stretching where a bittersweet relief is found. A place where we must pull ourselves back from the first-world, overabundance mentality and accept one all-important truth: life will be hard.

It will grow and stretch and threaten to break us in ways we cannot anticipate. It will bring the unexpected, the gut-punching, the downright hilarious in every season or chapter. The vehicle may be different, but the destination is the same.

Yes, our humanity will chafe against the truth of it. Seeking to find the best outcome, the deepest blessing, the happiest of endings on our own. But in all reality, we've already found what we think we must manufacture.

Jesus is the best outcome, the deepest blessing, the happiest of endings. He gives us the beauty, the grace, the rest we seek in the madness of real, messy life. And He gives us the safest of places to land when we break, when we rage, when we lose our ever-loving minds in the pain of this world.

Even though we tell ourselves that only in our striving can we taste His grace, the work of the Cross is enough, and it is the only good that will satisfy our souls.

So whatever you have faced, whatever you are facing, whatever you will face, know this . . .

He is good. He is faithful. He is but a breath away.

Even. When.

ACKNOWLEDGMENTS

To my precious friends and family, thank you for believing in me even on the days I couldn't believe in myself.

To my college bestie, Heather, thank you for kicking me in the can to just write the thing and giving me a quiet place to do so.

To Mary Southerland, thank you for cheering me on in my brokenness so I could be ready to write this from a place of healing.

To Edie Melson, thank you for reminding me of the beauty of perseverance, pressing forward, and never giving up.

To Paula Freeman, thank you for laying me at His feet so faithfully, for calling me friend, and for giving so freely of your skill as a writer.

To Michelle Cox, thank you for the early grace of your wisdom, expertise, and understanding of what it is to write with a body that's fussy.

To my agent and friend Blythe Daniel, thank you for seeing past my pandemic messiness and giving me the grace of a lifetime.

And to the entire Dexterity team, thank you for taking a chance on an unknown writer and for giving me the gift of a publishing team that feels like family.

ABOUT THE AUTHOR

Sara Cormany loves to see the grace of God in the messiest moments of life. She is the wife to one sweet guy and the mom to four beautiful kids. Sara uses her experiences as a mother, follower of Jesus, and someone living with chronic illness to inform her work as a writer and speaker.

Sara attended Cedarville University and received degrees in secondary education and communications. A speech educator for over twenty years, this teacher-turned-award-winning author is a lover of stories woven in everyday places. In addition to writing, she has worked as an editor, ghostwriter, coach, speaker, and project manager in the publishing industry. She has won and been a finalist for several Selah Awards for her articles and devotions, which have been published in *Fusion Family Magazine*, *Christian Devotions*, and more. She is on the faculty of several writing conferences, where she enjoys combining her training with her roles of author and speaker.

She also blogs about her experiences with life, loss, and everything in between on her website. A chronic illness fighter for over twenty years, she is honored to use her experiences to help others by leading a local support group for women with chronic and life-threatening illnesses. But no matter the chapter or season, Sara's journey is proof that a hard story can still be a good story.

Sara's family continues to inspire much of her writing. She lives with her husband and their four children in Kansas City, Kansas. She has contributed to multiple compilations and collaborative works, including *Born Beautiful: A Mother-Daughter Conversation on Beauty and Identity* and the award-winning *She Writes for Him: Stories of Living Hope. Even When* is Sara's first solo title. Join her at www.saracormany.com or on Facebook, Instagram, and Twitter as she chases babies, authentic faith, and Jesus.